To Chris ...
all my Be...

WINC___

AND THE BATTLE

by

BETTY BRAMMER

1970   1994

RICHARD KAY

80 SLEAFORD ROAD • BOSTON • LINCOLNSHIRE • PE21 8EU

For

PHILIP

and for

LINCOLNSHIRE

our land of many colours.

© Betty Brammer 1994

ISBN 0 902662 67 8

Typeset on an AppleMacintosh Plus and LaserWriter Plus using Microsoft Word and Aldus PageMaker

Printed by FOXE visual • Golf Road Industrial Estate • Mablethorpe • Lincolnshire • LN12 1NB

CONTENTS

Illustrations

ACKNOWLEDGEMENTS

Figs. 5, 9 and 14 have been reproduced from photocopies of old documents. Fig. 19 has been reproduced from *Boston and the Great Civil War* by A. A. Garner, [Richard Kay Publications 1972: reprinted 1992], for which it was specially drawn by Keith Bowler. Fig. 22 was drawn by Philippa Allday from sketches and information supplied by the author. All photographs of the present day have been taken for this book by the publisher except for that on the back cover for which we are indebted to the author's husband.

DRAMATIS PERSONAE — SOME OF THE NON-COMBATANTS INDIRECTLY INVOLVED IN THE BATTLE

(Regarding the Winceby villagers see also the following page)

Thomas Page, husbandman	d. 1673	Rev. Hugo Mapleson
Ann Page, his wife	d. 1679	William Barratt
Thomas Clarke	d. 1683	William Barratt, Jnr. (1668)
Robert Clarke		Moyses Barratt
William Thew		Richard Barratt d. 1667
William Hodgeson		Philip English d. 1689
Michael Briggs		Richard Couleman
John Burton (or Buxton)		Thomas Bardaile
Mary Burton (or Buxton)		Robert Spendley
Thomas Rutterforth		William Baudery
John Warner		William Houett
Helen Warner		George Barratt

CHILDREN OF WINCEBY (SOME OF THE)

****

Mairi Clarke	aged 14 yrs	Christopher Barratt		3 yrs
Thomas }	4 yrs	Richard }		3 yrs
Catharine }Page	2 yrs	William }Buxton	6 mths	
William }	11 mths	'daughter' }		2 yrs
Susanna Warner	5 mths	Thomas Kingston or Knighton	18 mths	

ELY
****

Elizabeth (Steward) Cromwell	mother	c. 1565-1654
Elizabeth (Bourchier) Cromwell	wife	c. 1597-1665
Bridget Cromwell	daughter	1624-1662
Richard Cromwell	son	1626-1712
Henry Cromwell	son	1628-1674
Elizabeth (Bettie) Cromwell	daughter	1629-1658
Mary Cromwell	daughter	1637-1713
Frances Cromwell	daughter	1638-1721
Major Henty Ireton, Deputy Governor of Ely garrison		c. 1611-1651

BOSTON
****

Richard Westland, Mayor of Boston
Rev Anthony Tuckney, Vicar of Boston
Thomas Coney, the Town Clerk

STICKNEY
****

Rev. Obadiah Howe, Vicar of Stickney

Some details of Winceby villagers living at the time of the battle, their antecedents and descendants, from the Parish register. The register is incomplete and, what there is, is not always readable. Included facts are accurate: omissions may or may not be so.

† Figures in brackets indicate ages at the time of the battle.

1613	William BARRATT	Baptised	(30)†
1617	George son of William BARRATT	Baptised	(26)
1627	Thomas son of William BARRATT	Baptised	(16)
1629	Mairi CLARK	Baptised	(14)
1632	Thomas PAGE & Anne EMPSON	Married	? May
1633	Anne dau. of Thos. & Anne PAGE	Baptised	22 Jan
1633	Anne wife of Thomas PAGE	Buried	24 Jan
1633	Anne dau. of Thomas PAGE	Buried	25 Jan
1635	Thomas PAGE & Ann CLARK	Married	June
1639	Thomas son of Thos. & Ann PAGE	Baptised	May (4)
1640	Christopher son of Thos. & Mary BARRATT	Baptised	April (3)
1640	Richard son of John & Alice BUXTON	Baptised	Jan (3)
1641	Catharine dau. of Thos. & Ann PAGE	Baptised	29 April (2)
1641	.... dau. of William BUXTON	Baptised	(2)
1642	William son of Thos. & Ann PAGE	Baptised	15 Nov(11 mnths)
1642	Thomas son of Thos. & Eliz. KNIGHTON	Baptised	18 Feb (18 mths)
1643	William son of John & Mary BUXTON	Baptised	16 April (6 mths)
1643	Susanna dau. of John & Helen WARNER	Baptised	4 May (5 mths)
1647	Nathaniel son of Thos. & Ann PAGE	Baptised	30 Jan
1667	William PAGE & Elizabeth BARRATT	Married	May
1668	William BARRATT (?Senior)	Buried	June
1671	Elizabeth dau. of William & Eliz. PAGE	Baptised	May
1672	Thomas PAGE	Buried	
1674	Thomas son of William PAGE	Baptised	May
1677	Ann daughter of " "	Baptised	April
1678	Elizabeth dau. of " "	Buried	May
1679	Nathaniel PAGE single man	Buried	(32)
1679	Ann Widow of Thomas PAGE	Buried	6 October
1680	Elizabeth dau. of Thos. & Eliz. PAGE	Baptised	Mar
1682	John PAGE single man	Buried	August
1684	John son of Wm. & Eliz. PAGE	Baptised	October
1687	Elizabeth dau. of Wm. & Eliz. PAGE	Baptised	January

Churchwardens of St. Mary's Church, Winceby: Richard Isaac CLARK   William PAGE

Thos. & Ann Page = Thomas (4) Catharine (2) William (11mths)
....

John & Helen Warner = Susanna (5mths)
....

Thomas & Mary Barratt = Christopher (3)
....

William Barratt (30)
George Barratt (26)
John & Alice Buxton = Richard (3)
....

John & Mary Buxton = William (6 mths)
....

William Buxton = Daughter (2)
....

Thomas & Elizabeth Kingston or Knighton = Thomas (18mths)
....

Clark, Thew, Bawdrey etc.,

vi.

EARL OF MANCHESTER

THE EASTERN ASSOCIATION ARMIES
****

Sgt.-Major -General Edward Montagu,
                the Earl of Manchester (1602-71)
Colonel Sir Francis Russell of Chippenham
Colonel Valentine Walton, Lieut. Governor of Kings Lynn.
Q.M. Gen. Bartholemew Vermuyden, Dragoon Commander
Sir William Harlakenden

CROMWELL'S HORSE
Colonel Oliver Cromwell, Colonel of Horse (1599-1658)
Capt Lieut. James Berry of Cromwell's own Troop
                                        (c.1610-91)
Major Edward Whalley, Cromwell's cousin
Captain John Disbrowe, Cromwell's brother in law
Captain Oliver Cromwell, Cromwell's son (1623-44)
Captain Valentine Walton, Cromwell's nephew
Captain Ayres,
Captain Margery,
Captain Swallow
Captain Samuel Porter,
Captain Adam Laurence.

THE NORFOLK HORSE
Sir Miles Hobart of Plumstead, K.B. Colonel of Horse,
                Norfolk and Suffolk. (d. after 1653)
Major Knight, Hobart's Infantry
Captain Johnson, Hobart's Dragoons
Captain SAMUEL Moody, Hobart's Dragoons

LINCOLNSHIRE
Francis, Lord Willoughby of Parham,
                Lord Lieut. and Colonel Lincs. Horse
John Cage, a soldier under Capt.JOHN Moody,
                buried Horncastle

THE YORKSHIRE HORSE
Sir Thomas Fairfax, Colonel of Yorkshire Horse (1612-71)
Sir William Fairfax (cousin), Colonel of Horse (d.1644)
Sir Henry Foulis, Bart., Buried at Boston (d.Oct.1643)
Colonel Thomas Morgan, of Fairfax's Dragoons (1604-79)
Captain Player, of Fairfax's cavalry

HULL
Lord Ferdinando Fairfax, Governor of Hull (1584-1648)
Lady Ann Fairfax, wife of Sir Thomas (d.1665)
Mary Fairfax, daughter of Sir Thomas (1638-1704)
Sir John Meldrum (1595-1645)

Captain Piggott of the *Undaunted*
Captain Haddock of the *Resolution*
Captain Moyer of the *Hercules*

EARL OF NEWCASTLE

William Cavendish, the Earl of Newcastle (1593-1676)
Colonel Sir John Henderson,
                Governor of Newark (d.1658)
Colonel Sir William Widdrington,
                Governor of Lincoln (1610-57)
Colonel Sir William Savile,
                Governor of Sheffield (1612-44)
Colonel Sir Ingram Hopton, Kt,
                of Armley, Yorks. Dragoons (1614-43)
Colonel Roger Portington (m. Joanna Hopton),
                Dragoons (1610-83)
Major Robert Portington (brother),
                wounded at Winceby (d.1660)
Colonel Robert Brandling (m. Helen, Hopton's widow),
                                        (1617-69)
Colonel Sir Robert Dallison, of Greetwell
Colonel Sir Wm. Pelham, of Brocklesby (1591-1644)
Captain William Westlyd, of Grimsby
Captain Husthwaite Wright, of Stallingborough
Cornet Thomas Westlyd, of Grimsby
Cornet Thomas Waters, of Brigsley
Lt.-Col. Sir George Bowes, killed at Winceby
Captain Abraham Marcham, killed at Winceby
Lieut. Godfrey, captured or killed at Winceby
Lt.-Colonel Ayres (or Eyres), captured at Winceby
Colonel St. George, captured 'in the water' at Winceby
Major Askew, captured 'in the water' at Winceby
Captain Vernatt (or Vernas), killed at Winceby
Colonel Carnaby, captured or killed at Winceby
'Master' (?Major) Wheeler, wounded at Winceby
Miles Hope, a soldier, killed at Winceby
Lieut.-Gen. Charles Cavendish, (1621-43)
                cousin of Newcastle (k. Gainsboro')
Colonel Sir Samuel Tuke, Lincs. (Cavendish's horse)

Entering Winceby today:
1 . . . from the south and east – from Bolingbroke or Mavis Enderby. Winceby House on the right.

2 . . . from the north and west – from Horncastle.

Winceby today, to the casual passer-by, hardly exists. If it were not for the road signs it would be quite possible to drive through the 'village' without realising that one had passed through any grouping of dwellings. The churches have disappeared from the village; there are no readily evident cottages nor smaller dwellings. There is Winceby House, a business centre; a garage and petrol filling station; and, on closer investigation, a few smaller dwellings and farms. There are a few trees but the overall impression is of an open, almost treeless, landscape, with some hedges in the distance and, to the NW of the Hammeringham road there is an elongated copse leading south-westwards from Slash Pingle. There is no longer a parish of Winceby but a combined parish of Winceby with Lusby: the 1991 census gave a combined population of 99 and a noticeboard in Snipedales nature reserve gives a population for Winceby of 'about thirty'. This is Winceby today.

3. Looking north-west across Slash Hollow. The photograph was taken from a position close to the indicated site of the gravel pit (see Fig. 22 on page 77). towards the Hammeringham boundary. The copse running south-westwards from Slash Pingle can be seen on the left in the middle-distance.

4. This was probably the battlefield—at the outset at least—viewed from: a). Slash Lane looking northwards from approximately the position of the left wing of Fairfax's troops (see Fig 22 page 77). b). Looking westwards from the approximate position of the left wing of Henderson's troops. The gradient is less evident in the photograph than in reality.

AUTHOR'S NOTE

THE NAME 'WINCEBY' usually conjures up thoughts of a Civil War battle. That momentary interest may then fade with the realisation that it all happened three and a half centuries ago and that most historians have only briefly acknowledged the event as important.

Was the battle important? Despite the few earlier setbacks, it proved to be a major success and a turn-about for the fortunes of Parliament. Their newly commissioned Eastern Association under the Earl of Manchester was a union of armies raised by the counties of East Anglia, the Fens, and Lincolnshire. It was no mere coincidence that the vigilant Cromwell and his troops had already been widely deployed in the area's defence. The Association's victory at Winceby confirmed Parliament's need for the large, itinerant army to bring territorial muscle into county defences; after two successful years of achievement, the Eastern Association was used as the basis for a New Model Army, with Sir Thomas Fairfax as its General.

Curiously enough, Cromwell appears never to have commented upon Winceby, which was the occasion when, as a mere colonel, he was first delegated to command the Eastern Association cavalry. Perhaps his dramatic encounter with the brave Sir Ingram Hopton marred the occasion?

Then there were the people who lived at Winceby in 1643, who were they and what happened to them?

When asked to look for more details of the Winceby battle, I was none too keen at first because I didn't expect to find very much. However, the first two discoveries changed my mind and I was hooked on the subject – for the next six years!

The first find was the Winceby parish register begun in 1579. It was a small, pocket sized, book almost illegible in parts, and here, in the parchment pages, I found the real seventeenth century people of Winceby, together with their families, their tragedies, and their blessings.

The name of Thomas Page occured several times in the

1.

register: his marriage, loss of wife and baby, then re-marriage and family baptisms all seemed as if they had been waiting patiently for my special attention. Finding his will and inventory of 1672 proved that Thomas, his wife, Ann, and their children had all lived through the battle and carried on living at Winceby until their deaths, many years later. I found no mention at all of any villager dying in the battle, but then the parish register was not used for several months and someone had removed part of the page anyway! Thomas' son, William, married a neighbour's daughter, Elizabeth Barratt, in 1667, and Ann Page's will, in 1679, leaves bequests to several grandchildren.

The inventories give a personal insight into their homes and belongings. Thomas's father, John Page, was a yeoman with servants. He had oxen, sheep, horses, cows, swine, a haywain and a plough, as well as 'all the graine growing in the fields'. A dozen silver spoons mentioned in John's inventory of 1628, appear again in both Thomas' and Ann's inventories but now depleted to only seven spoons. John's haywain and plough are also described in the same terms in each of the Pages' inventories, including William's in 1717. The Protestation Return of 1642 for Winceby was signed by 20 males, none refused.

The Winceby Terriers and Bonney's *Church Notes* describe the old church of St. Mary's with its thatched roof, steeple and bells, the position and rooms of the parsonage, barns, gardens and twenty-one acres of glebe lands.

My second find consisted of several microfilms of the original 'newspapers' or broadsheets, of 1643. In the rantings of these Royalist and Parliamentarian writers, 'Mercurius Aulicus', 'Mercurius Civicus', 'Mercurius Britanicus' and the *Passages in Parliament*, I was able to study all the conflicting news of September and October 1643, including the battle of Winceby. Gradually the truth began to emerge as I read and re-read all this fascinating, blatant propaganda, and cross-referenced it with previous letters written by Cromwell, and the battle reports of Manchester, Widdrington and others.

Close on the heels of this primary evidence, came the

5. *Facsimilie—much reduced.*

THE
PARLIAMENT
SCOUT

Communicating His Intelligence
TO THE
KINGDOME

From *Friday* the 13.of *October*, to *Friday* the 20. of *October*. 1643

Our Scout presents you in the first place with the Copie of a Letter from the Earle of *Manchesters* Armie, dated the thirteenth of *October*.

Sir, I wish you had seen what we saw yesterday of God in the use of meanes, and indeed I never saw more: Sir, Take this Narration of a remarkable victory, Monday my Lord advanced to *Bullinbroke* Castle, intending to take it if possible, thereby to force the parts about it from the continuall disturbance of the enemy, his army consisted of about three thousand horse,

R

and

3.

discovery of many Civil War 'Tracts' or booklets about certain occasions, including Richard Cotes' *A True Relation of the Late Fight . . .* Several libraries opened their safes to me and allowed me to read old manuscripts, and it is here that I must begin to mention some of these helpful people.

The libraries at Grimsby, Lincoln, Hull, and Horncastle were extremely helpful, revealing lots of valuable material without the slightest sign of impatience, and I am deeply grateful to their staffs. The tiny library of Hunstanton came up trumps with the Blomefield books, these helped me finally to establish the relationship between Sir Miles Hobart and Sir Ingram Hopton.

The staff of Boston Library: what can I say about them? For six years they have patiently obtained new books, old books, photocopies, reference books, and even wrestled with the American authorities to try and get copies for me of some seventeenth century letters. I really could not have got very far without their consistent help and encouragement, perhaps they are as relieved as I am that my work is finished!

Details of Winceby, such as registers, wills, inventories and terriers were to be found in the Lincoln Archives Office, whose patient staff were always available for help and to offer advice.

The people who have had a direct bearing on my research deserve a special mention, and there are very many of them. Perhaps I should try to keep them to a chronological order, for all these people were important to my work.

Beginning in 1987, Mr J. N. CLARKE of Belchford, who kindly advised me about the Civil War Tracts in Lincoln Library; Arthur A. GARNER, not only for his lecture and book *Boston and the Great Civil War* but for his assistance in locating the microfilms and his continued interest in my work. Arthur CREDLAND, Keeper of the Maritime Museum at Hull, for giving me his guidance on seventeenth century boats and river conditions for the evacuation of Fairfax's cavalry from Hull. Dave RYAN of Partizan Press for his *English Civil War Notes & Queries* (which are an inexhaustible mine of Civil War information) and the totally absorbing Military Lectures which he organises each year; the stimulating lectures by Andy

ROBERTSHAW of the National Army Museum, London; geological help from Michael BADLEY of Badley Ashton Associates, Winceby; Mr S. J. BUTTON of Boston and Mr Alec CHATER; Jonathan WEBB for his information on Hopton's visit to Sheffield.

The people of Winceby deserve my special thanks for their patience and understanding, especially Mr and Mrs P. BOURNE, Mr and Mrs J. ENDERBY, Mr LADLOW, Mrs PATCHETT; and Mr MASON of Hammeringham; Lionel GROOBY, the Warden at the time of Snipe Dales; and in Scrafield, Mr J. READ who located for me the 'old field of rushes' where the armour was found!

There were many journeys to make. A visit to both Hinchingbrooke House and the Cromwell Museum in Huntingdon; Cromwell's House at Ely; Old Bolingbroke village; the 'Living History Group' at Wilberforce House, and the staithes in Hull. Lincoln and Newark Museums, the little Naseby Museum, and the Guildhall Museum in Boston have all produced artifacts to view from the Civil War. It would have been inconceivable not to visit some of the Civil War re-enactment events by both the Sealed Knot and The English Civil War Society (of whom I am a 'Friend'). I shall not forget their help and the atmosphere of that great 'last' Battle of Naseby.

As a member of the Cromwell Association, I have been priviledged to use their library facilities and must thank Michael BYRD, the librarian, for his assistance; also Dr. Peter GAUNT, the chairman, for the offer of a memorial plaque at Winceby.

Thanks to Michael HONEYBONE for his advice on Local History research; to the W.E.A. for their 'Learning Journeys'; to the archivists of the Norfolk and the Suffolk Record Offices, and to all my friends and family, who have had to put up with the seventeenth century for the last six years.

I have tried to use only proven characters, facts, and dates in my work. My husband has patiently read and constantly challenged all my writing, so that if I couldn't prove it, I couldn't use it! However, some occasions have been treated to a liberal, and hopefully legitimate, degree of imagination, but only where it could be supported by probability and it is left to the reader to disprove these possibilities.

Having declared that everyone is a true character, I must admit that the messengers to and from Hull could not be identified, but it is accepted that they would have existed.

Oh, the 'young man' in Chapter One? Yes, of course he is a real person. He is my son who spent a thoughtful, wet afternoon at Winceby six years ago and who then cajoled me (with short-lived promises of help) into undertaking this research!

B.Brammer, 1993
Hubberts Bridge, Boston.

1.

THE YOUNG MAN LEFT BOURNE'S GARAGE and walked quickly back to his car which was parked beside the petrol pumps. While he had been in the shop the sky had become overcast and now there was a threat of rain hanging in the air. He also noticed a new stillness in his surroundings, there was no passing traffic, not even a tractor working in the fields or the distant noise of traffic on the main road over the hill. When he'd stopped here a few minutes ago, the trees on the other side of the busy road had been teeming with crows noisily flapping in and out of the top branches, arguing and screaming over territorial rights. Even they remained perfectly still now as they sat watching him in total silence.

He turned his back on the sinister, black shadows and sat down in the driving seat to check up on the area with a road map, then starting the engine, drove away, uneasily wondering why he had chosen to drive all the way here for petrol that he didn't really need. A few seconds later, he drove into the small car park belonging to Snipe Dales Nature Reserve; several times he had passed here and never even given it a thought, but why had he bothered to make a special journey today?

The young man locked his car and went across to look at the Information Boards which were covered with maps, notices, and a description of the area. While he stood reading them a steady drizzle of rain began to fall, reminding him of the shelter his car offered. In the grey, wet mist the car looked warm and inviting, perhaps he should drive away and come back again when the weather was better.

Fastening his jacket and turning up the collar, he shrugged off the temptation to go back to his car and stepped

6. In the car park at Snipedales

out into a small lane which was narrow and quiet. Setting off at a brisk pace he followed the lane until it led him to a gate with another notice board next to it announcing briefly that the Battle of Winceby had taken place here on 11 October 1643, an important Civil War battle between the Royalists led by Colonel Henderson and the Parliamentarians led by the Earl of Manchester. The Royalist army suffered heavy losses of men in a tragic massacre.

'That date', the youth thought wryly, 'should be easy enough for me to remember. I was born on 11 October – three hundred and ten years later!'

Intrigued by the coincidence of the date, he went through the gate and walked until he reached a clearing amongst the trees where there were a few old tombstones sheltering under the branches of a large tree. Some were very old and sadly neglected but a search amongst them told him nothing apart from the obvious fact that these were the graveyard ruins of a long-gone Church. The graveyard was situated very close to the edge of a small cliff and he could see cattle grazing in the fields down below, a dog was barking, cattle were lowing in the distant farm buildings and somewhere there was a tractor engine running. Perhaps there really was nothing out of the ordinary here in this peaceful, summer countryside.

Making his way back through wet grass and nettles to the footpath he continued on his ramble and eventually found himself standing at the side of a small ravine. It had steep banks that plunged downwards into a fast running beck where the water could be heard splashing around the rocks below and lapping against the sides of the bank; as water was pumped steadily uphill to the farm, vibration from the hydraulic ram seemed to give a rhythmic heartbeat to the earth beneath his feet.

Sheltered from the rain by the trees he stood and gazed at the natural beauty of the valley, a magic refuge where birds, insects and wild flowers were protected and allowed to flourish in safety. He let his mood drift with the peace of the valley until its remote sadness reminded him of those who had lived and died here. It seemed incredible to him that this tiny hamlet of Winceby had once been a battlefield and the cause of a significant turning point in history. Suddenly he realised that this tragedy had become commonplace, its importance was already diminished by the brevity of history books and yet somewhere, with diligent research, there must be such a lot to discover about the battle, the men who fought it, and the inhabitants who witnessed it. There and then he decided that the truth would have to be uncovered, little by little and with some help, he would see that the full story emerged to occupy its own important place in history.

It was as if a great worry had been lifted from his mind, the decision was made and the sooner he began his task, the better. Deep in thought he left the valley and returned to the car park, where he took off his wet coat and then sank thankfully into the driving seat of his car. The young man began to wonder what this place had looked like in 1643. Like all of the fields in Winceby, the car park was surrounded by hedges which surely could not have been here when the battle was fought. He tried to visualise the incredible sight of thousands of men with all their banners, weapons and horses, converging on this quiet, little village, but it proved difficult for the tidy fields and the modern roadway were almost impossible to ignore.

He sat for a while longer, enjoying the peace as he allowed his imagination to work on removing all visible traces of the last three and a half centuries. First of all, he decided that the road would have to go, its smooth tarmac surface, cat's eyes and markings would look incongruous in the 17th century. Perhaps a well-trodden highway with ruts left by carts and carriage wheels, some hastily repaired pot-holes and churned over mud in the wet weather? The buildings would have to go, of course. He would clear away the modern bungalows, the nineteenth century Winceby House and the rectory before tackling the hedges; crops, animals, and the people could not be disposed of so easily. He would need to think more carefully about these. . . .

*   *   *   *   *

Over Winceby the sky darkened and the hour grew late, its buildings began to vanish – and so did the farm! Up on the higher ground near the hidden ravine, other smaller, cottages returned to their old positions, they were made of mud and stud or stone and most had neatly thatched roofs.

The hedges that had surrounded each of the fields shrank away transforming much of the village into an open countryside deeply contoured by the sloping wold hills. A small, thatched church with a steeple took up its place by the churchyard which now contained different tombstones. The little, thatched parsonage, its barn and outbuilding set in an acre of land between the church on the east and Mark Hill to the north west, became visible once again. There were many footpaths leading from cottages to the church, a few led further afield into Lusby, Hagworthingham, Scrafield, Hammeringham and other villages nearby.

In the pale moonlight a tall boundary hedge, dense with vicious thorns, left a dark shadow as it snaked across the hill and raced away into the distant night. Where the boundary hedge abutted gates that crossed over muddy lanes, its shadow skipped and then carried onwards, weaving and turning as it

10.

made a protective cordon around Winceby.

The air now had a sharper chill to it and daylight would show leaves on the trees, no longer a fresh green but coloured in autumn tints. The wild, summer flowers growing amongst the trees were also gone, replaced by berries and ferns. While the young man watched, the modern, summer-time Winceby was rapidly changing before his fascinated gaze into the autumn of 1643.

The sound of a dog growling close behind made him jump and he turned sharply to discover that he was now sitting on a pile of logs beside the door of a thatched, stone cottage. When its occupant opened the door, a dog raced out and ran straight past the young man into the moonlit garden, only to stand there and bark at an intruder he couldn't see!

Thomas Page called his dog back into the cottage and then, unaware of the youth sitting beside him, he stayed a while in the doorway to listen to the night sounds which were no longer the agreeable noises he was used to hearing on the Winceby hillside. Before the troubles began he could have stood here and listened to the wind blowing through the trees, bending their branches and hurling the dead leaves round and round the cottage. The leaves would patter against the door and window shutters as the wind swirled them around in a frenzy. In the morning, Thomas would gather the leaves up so that Ann would not complain about them treading into the cottage. The dry leaves burnt well, and packed down over the herbs and roots in the garden they would also help to keep some of the winter frosts at bay. Most evenings he would stand and listen to the water rushing down the ravine. Sometimes in the summer, it would trickle past in a loving, playful mood, causing no damage to the banks and leaving the path dry and safe to walk on.

In a momentary lull, he heard again the screeching of an owl as it pounced upon its prey, closely followed by the cackle of a startled pheasant, out of touch with its mate and calling for direction. Nowadays these sounds at Winceby were drowned by the noise of men's voices, their shouts, bursts of laughter and singing, the neighing of the cavalry horses and, more fearfully, the sounds of musket shot and cannonfire.

All these noises echoed here from the royal village of Bolingbroke which was two miles away and situated at the base of some folds in the hills. The village was built around an old castle, the birthplace of King Henry IV and now used as an army garrison. The Royalists were holding the castle in preparation for the arrival of their forces which were now steadily advancing on Lincolnshire from the north.

Thomas Page, listening to all these intrusive sounds, leaned against his cottage door and sighed. This war seemed to threaten them all, he could feel an unfriendly keeness in the wind, even the moon looked whiter and colder than before. The long winter was close at hand and even without a war it was well able to threaten their survival once again.

Suddenly, he felt that he was not alone and called softly into the darkness. No one moved or answered him. He turned and looked quickly at the dog lying quietly on the ground, apparently asleep. Thomas stepped back into the cottage and closed the door, then pushed the bolt across carefully before hurrying back again into the warmth of his bed and Ann's arms.

The dog did not move. He appeared to be asleep, though had Thomas Page stayed to look at him more carefully he would have noticed that the hackles on the back of the dog's neck stood up like the spines of a hedgehog!

Outside, the young man moved away from the cottage and treading carefully to avoid Ann's herb garden, he wandered off in the direction of a lane that crossed through the centre of Winceby. He found it an exciting experience seeing the village as it was in 1643, so unlike the tidy, cultivated scene he'd left, but there was something worrying him, nagging at his sub-conscious thoughts and he needed to think about it. The information he sought was here. Already he'd met one of the villagers and this was just what he had wanted, wasn't it? He stopped and looked around him, what was wrong here and why should he be so uneasy? The moon bathed the hills and village with its brightness, allowing him to study the sleeping village. Suddenly he realized what was wrong, he'd arrived BEFORE the battle, not afterwards!

The shock hit him with such force that he sank onto his

knees clutching his stomach as he fell...Dear God! Not that! He didn't want to be a witness to the battle. That was not what he was after, just to know the true story would be enough.

The young man groaned, understanding how blind he had been. Somehow, he'd lost control of the situation and was now totally committed to this crazy, impulsive search. He stood upright and took a deep breath, then another, for he badly needed courage to see him through the revelations of this night.

He experienced a touch of panic when some of the shadows beneath the trees began to move about, there was a movement too in the dark corners of the boundary. Surely he ought to go now and leave them in peace? Even as the thought entered his head he was aware of the answer, these shadows needed his testimony and were waiting for him to acknowledge them.

*   *   *   *   *   *

Standing alone in the middle of the battlefield, the young man raised his head and held out his arms to the darkness surrounding him. With a voice trembling with emotion he called out to the swirling shadows, imploring them to come forward and help him with the telling of their story. Then, as if he knew what was required of him, the young man turned and walked slowly back to the head of the ravine where he climbed upon one of the huge boulders - and waited.

Silently and obediently his ghosts stepped forward, ready to re-live their memories for him, and even to die once more for true recognition. In their thousands they came to the muster, bringing with them a variety of muskets, pistols, swords and pieces of armour. Some led their frightened horses onto the battlefield, others proudly carried their silken colours, decorated with emblems and words of glory that blazed like fire in the bright moonlight.

For a few fleeting moments they remained visible to him, then melting into the darkness again, they went in search of the place where it all began. . . .

2.

T HE HAMLET OF WINCEBY supported very few families, probably due to its position high on a layer of sandstone that ran through the southern edges of the Lincolnshire Wolds, the ridge of hills that ran north westward from nearby Spilsby to Caistor. The porous sandstone lying on top of a firm clay bed caused springs to seep out forming a watershed that often flooded its lower ground. Consequently, the villagers confined most of their homes to the higher, dry ground near the top of a hidden ravine. The road from Horncastle to Spilsby cut through the village on the higher ground, another branched southwards towards Bolingbroke and the fens. There wasn't a great deal here to offer a large community – in medieval times Winceby had become one of many deserted villages.

Thomas Page, a husbandman of Winceby, was working on the roof of his cottage, he was in a contented mood, enjoying one of the last few sunny days left before the coming winter started. The roof had started to let rain in recently so he was anxious to repair the damage while the weather held good. From the heights of Winceby there was a magnificent view over the flatness of the East Fen, stretching as far south as the town of Boston with its distant silhouette of St. Botolph's famous landmark just visible on the skyline. The castle at Tattershall and Lincoln cathedral were also visible on a clear day. On his roof, Thomas could look across to the thatched roof of the tiny village church with its stones and wooden crosses crowding the graveyard below.

Taking a moment's rest from his work, he sat back on his heels and let his thoughts go back to the summer day when he and Anne Empson were married, they were young and happy for such a very brief time. In the bitterly cold January of the following year little Anne was prematurely born, then quickly baptised before she died. The next day her mother also died. Over there by the church wall in a quiet corner of the graveyard they both rested peacefully, undisturbed by all the troubles of today.

In nearby Bolingbroke there was no peace at all and quite certainly no rest from the army that had besieged the castle since Monday. All the villages in the area had resounded with the noise of recent Parliamentary attacks on the Royalist garrison though, strangely, today had been different. This morning's sounds consisted mainly of frequent trumpet calls, drumming, and orders being shouted. Thomas wondered if the army of Parliament was going back to Boston, leaving them all to settle down again to a quieter life.

7. Looking from Winceby over the East and West Fens towards Boston. It is just possible to discern the almost 280 foot high tower of St. Botolph's church—some 15 miles distant— in the centre on the horizon.

After his wife's death, life still had to go on for Thomas and so two years later his name was once again written into the little book of St. Mary's church when he and Ann Clarke had their June wedding. He smiled happily to himself as he thought of the three little ones down below him in the cottage. Young Thomas was four years old, Catherine was two and a half and William, eleven months old. William had played with the two older children since day-break and was now in his cot enjoying the sleep of the exhausted whilst Ann was busy drying some fruit and herbs.

With his work on the roof nearly complete, Thomas decided that if the army was moving on, it would be safe to take the family on a visit down to Horncastle market next week. While they were there they could visit his aunt who would spoil the children, marvel at how they had grown this summer and send them all homeward with their bellies full of her very special hot broth.

Although it would take days for the children to settle down again after the excitement Ann would love the outing and hear all the latest gossip and news from his aunt. This summer had been a very poor one with more rain than usual and they had not ventured far from home with the children. Perhaps before he mentioned the outing he should wait and see if the weather held fair until next week.

Looking towards the boundary hedges near Hammeringham and Scrafield he could see how badly the land was still waterlogged. Along the banks of the East Beck and the Hannah Beck tall rushes would normally grow, but nowadays all that could be seen of these rushes were their broken tips, bending with the flowing river and apparently growing in the middle of a steaming, boggy lake. Only the roads and the higher ground were safe just now.

The midday sun was quite strong for October and he needed to shield his eyes as he turned to look around at the homes of his friends and neighbours. There were cottages scattered near to the footpaths leading to and from the church. He could just make out the cottage of John Buxton in the distance and the Barratts lived fairly near but were hidden by the trees.

At this time of year the trees were full of colours with their dying leaves having changed into beautiful shades of gold, red, orange and blue.

Blue? Thomas stiffened as he saw the blue silk moving about amongst the trees and seconds later saw a great mass of cavalry approaching from the direction of Bolingbroke. Troops of cavalry riding through Winceby on a look-out for the enemy and foraging for supplies were a familiar sight for the local people – this was not. There was a more ominous size and sound in the slow advance of these horses. Threatening and wary, they pressed onward towards the village.

Turning to look behind him, Thomas groaned as he saw yet more coloured silks flying on the skyline of the distant hill and approaching them from the opposite direction – from Horncastle. Shock ran through Thomas's body as he realised the awful truth of what he was watching. He attempted to stand up but his legs seemed to have gone numb and when he tried to shout a warning, his dry throat could only croak. Although it seemed like minutes to him, Thomas's brain only took a couple of seconds to function again before he began shouting a warning at the top of his voice. Hastily leaving the roof, he clattered down the ladder at lightening speed, and lost his balance at the bottom!

Panic and noise quickly turned into chaos at the home of the Page family. There was a full chorus of sounds in which Catherine's terrified screams figured quite prominently, while William's sudden, awakening cries almost managed to drown the worried shouts of his mother – who thought Thomas had fallen from the roof. When Ann trod on the dog's paw as she rushed outside, the injured animal limped about adding his frenzied howls to the clamour.

Young Thomas, unable to compete with his sister's screams, watched silently as his father appeared to behave like a madman racing about and shouting at them, telling them to get away from their home as fast as they could. The child's bottom lip began to tremble as sudden fear and confusion swept over him, tears welled up in his eyes and then rolled slowly down his cheeks.

So fell the first of all the tears that were to be shed in Winceby that day.

All this commotion served to alert some neighbours who duly ran to the church and began ringing the two church bells and the Sanctus bell as a warning, drawing the attention of the villagers to the dangers of remaining in the path of two opposing armies.

After most of the families had been alerted and gathered together, it was agreed that the women and children would have to take shelter near the ravine. Its crevasses stretched out from beyond Lusby and were shaped like the grasping fingers of a hand clutching at the Winceby Hills. Full of trees and undergrowth, the head of the ravine had steep, muddy banks dropping down to a swollen river, in some places almost two hundred feet below. Beyond the ravine, the ground dropped away less steeply, forming valleys of arable land between the 'fingers' and so leaving a few secure ledges where

8. A suitable place of refuge for the Winceby villagers during the battle. There are several similar 'safe' places. This is within a few yards of the site of St Margaret's church.

the villagers could take cover. It seemed to be the most likely place for an army to avoid during a battle.

Out of the initial chaos there evolved an instinctive group

18.

organisation. The evacuating groups were to take with them all the possessions they could safely carry. The older children held hands tightly with the toddlers and coaxed them to hurry, the girls supported their aged grandparents and the sick, while the women collected and carried huge bundles of possessions wrapped in bed-covers. Pewter dishes and brass pots rattled together in sacks as their owners hurriedly gathered them up.

In the meantime, the men were bolting doors and fastening the window shutters, others rounded-up as many animals as they could, carefully herding them into the already overcrowded Deepdale pasture at the lower end of the ravine. Most of the swine and poultry had been taken down to the valleys and hidden as soon as the Royalist troopers at the castle began foraging amongst the local villages. The older boys were hurriedly trying to move precious bushels of barley, malt and oats to safety and helping the very young and the infirm to negotiate muddy tracks. Ann's fourteen year old sister, Mairi, trundled away with baby William sitting astride her hip (still screaming his head off) and clasping five month old Susanna Warner tightly to her bosom. Behind her, Mary Buxton was carrying her own baby son William and having trouble with two young toddlers who wanted to sit down and play.

Protection in the shape of scythes, hedge slashers and long knives had not been forgotten and armed with these a line of defence formed in front of the refuge. Old William Barratt refused to leave his home, declaring that he would use the wood-chopper on any soldier who tried to enter. One of his grandsons ran to fetch the defiant hero's son George, a hefty lad who simply picked up the old man as if he were a baby and carried him off to join the others. He was content to stay there when a neighbour offered him a bundle of bedding to rest on while he watched the impending conflict from his ringside seat.

With Thomas's fortunate warning many of the anxious spectators had been given time to evacuate their homes, but there were still stragglers arriving in from their plots of land, hastily glancing behind in fear of pursuit and many out of breath after chasing scattered sheep.

One of the churchwardens, Christopher Clarke, had gone to help the Rector, Hugo Mapleson. Together, they went into the little Norman church and hurriedly gathered up the pewter flagon and plate, the Elizabethan chalice, two handbells and a laten cross; books, old documents and the church register were bundled hastily into the parish chest until it could hold no more. With the poor-box carefully tucked under the Rector's arm, they set off to safety, dragging the heavy chest behind them. When he managed to reach the ravine, the Rector was needed immediately to try and calm the sick and the frightened, who were certain that they would either be killed by the soldiers or fall into the river and drown.

*   *   *   *   *   *

Advancing from Bolingbroke, the Parliamentarian army appeared to be without any infantry support and consisted entirely of troopers and dragoons. It had just passed the village and was beginning to ascend the hill towards Scrafield, when the full mass of Royalist colours now assembling on the horizon in front of them, became fully visible to the Parliamentary scouts.

Trumpets sounded an alarm as scouts belatedly sent the frantic warning, that these were not just one or two of the usual Royalist scouting troops watching them from the hilltop, but a whole army that was on the march and coming to relieve the siege of Bolingbroke castle!

The advancing Parliamentary army was brought to an immediate halt and everyone waited impatiently while the senior officers assembled and then seemed to give an exaggerated performance of consultation. Suddenly, a triumphant cheer arose from the group of spectators at the top of the ravine. To the astonishment of all and the dismay of its own cavalry troops, a portion of the leading regiment of the Parliamentary army appeared to perform an about-turn, as if to make an orderly retreat back to Boston.

The delighted locals were still dancing, waving and jeering at the retreating soldiers when a tremendous shout of 'Cavendish' silenced them. A few of the Royalist cavalry troops charged downhill after the withdrawing troops fully expecting to put their enemy to a run and so rout them. Their dire shouts threatened blood, victory and most of all – Revenge!

As the rest of the Royalist army began its descent, carelessly leaving behind all the advantages of their hilltop position, a signal from the Colonel in charge of the Parliamentary troops brought his assumed retreat to a sudden halt, springing the trap shut just as his enemy was approaching level ground.

All hopes of routing the enemy faded when the Royalist leaders realised that they had been duped by the enemy's strategy into leaving the hill. Thomas also knew, standing amongst his dismayed neighbours and watching the two armies surveying their positions, that his first gut reaction had been correct.

There *would* be a battle and it was going to be fought right here in his innocent village – may God help them all!

3.

A Time to Begin . . .

. . . WITH THE EASTERN ASSOCIATION

T HE TWO ARMIES SURVEYED EACH OTHER and then began drawing up into their battle formations. As usual, there was no hurry or panic, the fighting would not begin until both sides were ready, and it would take more than an hour to get thousands of men and horses into position.

Each side counted the other's number of colours flying, the Royalists had seventy four cavalry colours and another twenty one for the Dragoons, making ninety five in all. Although the Parliamentarians appeared to have barely fifty colours in all, it was noticed that their troops were fuller than the Royalists and were therefore not so heavily out-numbered.

Colonel Oliver Cromwell of the Parliamentary horse leaned forward across his saddle and stroked the graceful arch of his horse's neck, then absent-mindedly fingered its mane as he watched the enemy drawing up their divisions. Immediately behind him, his cavalry troops were busy arranging their positions, trumpets vibrating over the bustle as they sounded the colours. He could also hear the faint, intermittent beating of drums at Bolingbroke almost two miles behind them, where the Infantry were being pressed to hurry along.

While he was waiting for a message to arrive from his commander, the Earl of Manchester, the Colonel mused over the last fifteen months and its drastic events. England had been plunged into a state of civil war when the autocratic King Charles I challenged Parliament and raised his Standard at Nottingham in August 1642. Like thousands of other men Cromwell had to learn how to fight and kill, not a foreign enemy but his own countrymen, even his friends and neighbours.

Only the previous year, on 23rd October, 1642, the first

shocking battle of Edgehill had proved just how unprepared the country was for such an occasion. On both sides there were many officers experienced in foreign war commanding men who were unwilling and untrained. That indecisive and tragic battle had demonstrated a need, especially in the Parliamentarian army, for equipping and training good fighting men. Old family retainers and vagrants were no use in serious combat.

Cromwell recognised the problem. He had learnt quickly, for soon after holding a commission in a foot regiment, he became captain of his own troop of cavalry, number sixty-seven in the Earl of Essex's army.

Experience had taught him the importance of careful recruiting, good equipment and above all, discipline. Today he had his own efficient regiment of ten cavalry troops, hand-picked men who were brave and God-fearing enough to rely on in the heat of battle. Only one year after Edgehill, Cromwell had earned his position as one of the five Colonels of Horse in the Eastern Association army, and was now preparing to lead the General's troops, as well as his own, into the ensuing battle.

The Colonel allowed himself a grim smile, satisfied that the enemy had been drawn so successfully into the trap, their leaders had chased here and there throughout Lincolnshire, lured by tantalising glimpses of the bait; though the business had not been without its dangers and close-shaves. Cromwell turned in his saddle and looked back at Sir Thomas Fairfax who was also watching the opposing army very closely; this was the day they had waited for, and with God's help the end of the day should prove them right.

There was still no message from the Earl of Manchester. Cromwell knew the Infantry were on the way from Bolingbroke and anxious to arrive in time to support him, although the climb from the village would prove a steep and tortuous journey for the ordnance waggons, especially if they became bogged down in the mud. Even the soldiers carrying muskets or pikes would find the uphill march an arduous task.

When he turned back to look at the Royalists, Cromwell noted that they were apparently still re-positioning some of their ranks. Relaxing a little, he recalled his recent introduction to Fairfax, or 'Black Tom' as the devoted Yorkshire troopers called him. It had been only a matter of two or three weeks since they had first met. The Parlimentarian city of Hull had been under siege by William Cavendish, Earl of Newcastle, who, with his large Royalist army was attempting to capture the vital port for the King.

At the same time much further south, the Earl of Manchester, recently commissioned by Parliament as Sergeant Major General of the Eastern Association army, was laying siege to the Royalist held port of Kings Lynn. The besieged Royalists in Lynn gave little resistance and capitulated on September 16th, thus enabling Manchester and his army to concentrate on defending Lincolnshire against the expected advance of Newcastle and his Royalist troops. Manchester despatched some troops and supplies to Colonel Cromwell and ordered him to march northwards to Barton on Humber, where he was to organise the evacuation of Sir Thomas Fairfax and his cavalry from Hull, then escort them all safely back to Boston.

It was a memorable occasion. The Colonel and his army had set out from Boston about the 18th of September, their route taking them along the top of the Wolds where its high ridges offered the cavalry an excellent surveillance over the surrounding open countryside. Cromwell sent an advance party to Barton on Humber to begin the ferry preparations and arrange quarters for the men. Barton was a small town with a massive Saxon tower, fine churches and narrow streets; news of this army approaching them caused a surge of increased activity amongst all the provision merchants and boat-owners.

With the development of such an important port as Hull on the opposite side of the river, Barton functioned as a busy ferry taking various merchandise across the River Humber for export to the Continent, and returning again with valuable imports ordered by the southern traders. Here on the river shoreline, a mile or so from the town of Barton, lay a variety of boats moored to dozens of jetties, while others waited amongst the creeks in the salt marshes and on the beaches along the coast.

There were sturdy, flat-bottomed wooden craft, medium sized trading vessels, sprit-rigged and measuring up to thirty-five feet in length, all with a shallow draft for beaching. These were the ideal vessels for ferrying horses across the river from Hull to Barton, and Cromwell's officers were busily impressing into service all the owners they could muster of serviceable craft. Many haggled over payment, but by and large some agreement had to prevail because the goodwill of the experienced river men was so essential for a smooth and successful evacuation.

Cromwell recalled how he very soon had cause to regret that the General had not allocated him a much larger escort for the campaign. There were regular sightings of Royalist troops, his scouting parties had seen the enemy crossing the river Trent and they were known to be heading towards Barton. Apart from sending a message back about their situation, there was little else they could do other than prepare defences and get the two thousand horses, troops and baggage away from Hull as quickly as possible. Leaving his senior officers to carry on with the preparations, Colonel Cromwell stepped aboard one of the boats waiting to cast off and, accompanied by his personal guard, crossed the river Humber to meet with the Fairfaxes in Hull.

The boat journeyed swiftly down the river Humber, conveying with its military passengers the cargo of supplies stacked below decks for the garrison. From a distance the entire city of Hull appeared to be surrounded by a huge wall with many half-moon batteries and fortresses interspaced along its span, like a jewelled necklet. Behind these battlements rose the high rooftops of many fine, large buildings, the white landmark tower of the jail and several church spires, one of them much taller than the others.

Cromwell was impressed by the sight of Hull's remarkable defences. There were siege works in front of the western walls and away to the right of the city stood a huge blockhouse with its Parliamentary flag flapping proud defiance over the river. While marvelling at the strength of the city's fortifications, the boat passed a 'man-o-war' anchored in the river, one of several ships keeping an ever watchful eye along the river and its banks for signs of an attacking enemy. Already alerted to the impending evacuation plans, the ships received and passed signals between each other as well as conveying messages between shore parties.

The boat headed for the Humber landing place, a south–facing, triangular piece of land that jutted out into the river. This landing place was the most convenient one for ferries, the area being flat and, apart from the ducking stools at one side, less cluttered than the protected Haven.

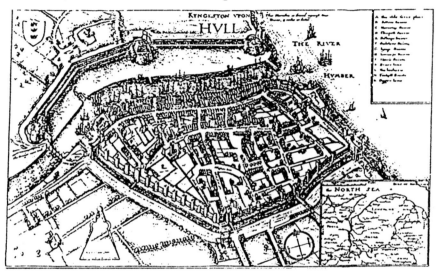

9. Hull can be seen to be almost surrounded by massive fortifications. Note the orientation showing north to the left. Although too small to see in this greatly reduced reproduction the dividers represent 200 yards ('600 foote'). [Engraving by W. Hollar 1640]

Immediately past this jetty was the busy entrance to the River Hull where dozens of small cargo boats were negotiating their way in and out of the crowded Haven, jostling with each other to unload their stores at the various High Street staithes.

Waiting to welcome the visitors, and accompanied by his senior officers, was Sir Thomas Fairfax, a tall, thin faced man with large dark eyes and a fine black moustache. He was dressed in the uniform of a cavalry officer and sported a red montero hat on top of his shoulder-length black curls. Sir Thomas was the son of Lord Ferdinando Fairfax, the Governor of Hull and defender of the city against Newcastle's powerful

26.

Royalist army.

Cromwell was already aware of Sir Thomas's reputation for great courage and daring in battle, so the warm welcome that he now received from this courteous young gentleman helped to lay the foundation of respect and trust needed for their military achievements. The two Fairfaxes, father and son, had fought valiantly to hold Yorkshire for Parliament, but against the mighty army of the Earl of Newcastle they had faced overwhelming odds. After many brave stands including Leeds, Wakefield, and Selby, the Fairfaxes had at last been forced to retreat here into Hull, where they were now surrounded on three sides by the enemy.

Amongst the officers waiting with Sir Thomas were his Lieut. Colonel of Horse, Sir Henry Foulis, and also his cousin Sir William Fairfax, both men of hard fighting experience. The visitors were accompanied from the landing place and taken through the Watergate entrance into Hull, a tiny postern which led under an old archway into the very narrow Little Lane. The narrow lane was designed especially to restrict enemy access in the event of a river attack. Life in the city appeared to be reasonably normal as the inhabitants bustled about their daily chores, confident in the security of the defences. Hull's governor took no uneccessary risks, by controlling all the city's supplies and functions, his officers were able to ensure law and order both day and night.

As well as securing a home for the townspeople, the garrison had many duties to perform. It was a refuge from the enemy, a training ground for recruits and a hospital for casualties, a haven for the boats, magazine and equipment, a base from which to mount raiding parties, and a prison. Supplies were unloaded from the mass of cargo boats in the River Hull and were passed across from one boat to another under the close scrutiny of military guards.

All the city gates were manned continuously by sentinels. To avoid any collusion with spies from the outside (and there had been several attempts) the sentries were drawn by lots at the last minute; the password was never written down but whispered to each other before going on watch. To make sure that the word was correctly heard and understood, it was whispered back again to the Major by the last man!

During their meeting, Lord Fairfax told Cromwell that he was confident Hull was secure enough to withstand the siege, but only if this constant vigilance against treachery could be maintained. The city was greatly overcrowded with soldiers billeted in every home, many families temporarily gathered together in one larger house and left their own empty houses to be filled by the army. The city relied entirely on supplies coming in from the sea but some foods were often in short supply, causing occasional 'fasting days.' There was plenty of grain imported into the city for bread, the difficulty was in grinding it quickly enough to supply everyone.

Fresh drinking water was one of the first things cut off by the Royalists. The wells inside the defences were sufficient to cater for the population, but it became a more serious problem with an army present. The cavalry horses were suffering during the siege, many became very ill through drinking the only available supply for animals and some died from the stale, brackish water. For the besieged city, such an excess of cavalry became a heavy burden. To the Eastern Association army, trying to prevent the threat of Newcastle's army sweeping through Lincolnshire towards London, a bonus of these twenty-one Cavalry troops would be of tremendous value.

Inside the Governor's mansion house and seated round a huge refectory table now covered with official documents, maps and defence sketches, the Fairfaxes discussed military strategy, past battles and political problems together with Cromwell and several other senior officers. They were eager to hear all his news, even though the Parliamentary situation was rapidly becoming serious now that London was threatened by the Royalist advances. Word that the Scottish professional soldier, Colonel Sir John Meldrum, would soon be returning to Hull with five hundred soldiers was greeted with more enthusiasm. The spirits of the group raised as they drank wine and talked of lifting the siege, defeating Newcastle and turning the tide for Parliament. Plotting by the fireside, the glimmer of a plan emerged that just might, with careful strategy, lift the siege of Hull and prevent the Royalists from taking Lincolnshire.

The Earl of Newcastle's army was divided at the present time because some of the forces who advanced southwards with him in August to capture Gainsborough had wanted to return home in order to harvest their crops, and so refused to stay. The Earl had returned north to besiege Hull, leaving garrisons at Sheffield, Newark and Gainsborough to continue with the march south through Lincolnshire.

The Royalists had made many sorties further into the county and provided garrisons at Bolingbroke Castle and Wainfleet Haven in readiness for their anticipated capture of the fenland regions. If the Royalists could be drawn into marching to the assistance of one of their outposts under siege in Lincolnshire, then Manchester might be persuaded to use his newly augmented army and engage the enemy – whilst Hull tried to free itself! Arrangements were made for safer communications between Hull and Boston, codes were agreed for names, dates and places and a provisional estimation of time needed was discussed.

Lord Ferdinando's wife had died in childbirth in 1619 when Thomas was only seven years old, but Cromwell was able to meet Lady Anne Fairfax, the wife of Sir Thomas. Lady Anne was a loyal wife, as the daughter of a general she was already used to military life and bravely followed her husband to look after and nurse him. Sir Thomas was not always in good health having contracted malarial fever during the fighting in the Netherlands war, but it was his extraordinary daring on the battlefield that caused his wife the most anxiety. When the battle got started and the going got tough, 'Black Tom' Fairfax became totally fearless, outfaced tremendous odds and inspired his men to even greater courage than they actually possessed. He received many wounds, some very severe, and she helped him to survive them all.

Only recently, Sir Thomas and his cousin Sir William Fairfax, together with Sir Henry Foulis who had been wounded at Seacroft, had to fight their way out of besieged Bradford with the aid of only fifty troopers. Lady Anne Fairfax was travelling with them on horseback and seated behind one of their servants.

It was just after they had left Bradford when the Fairfaxes

were attacked by three hundred Royalists, Sir Thomas and his men fought their way through them, then turning to look back at the enemy, saw that Lady Anne and William Hill the servant had been captured! Fairfax had been quite sure that his wife would come to no harm, although these men were the enemy, many of them were once his friends, local neighbours and landowners who now fought for his cousins on the King's side. Sure enough, Lady Anne was released and then restored to her husband in Hull by the courtesy of Newcastle, who loaned her his own coach in which to travel.

A tour of the city's defences was arranged for Cromwell and his officers the next day. Of prime interest was the massive brick wall built about three hundred years earlier around three sides of the city. At their foundations the walls were approximately 4ft 6ins thick and rose about 14ft high to a parapet walkway. During their tour of the north and west defences, Cromwell surveyed the massive interval towers, 29ft high and oblong shaped, four of them having well-guarded gatehouses with drawbridges built into them.

Leaving the north gatehouse, they rode down High Street and cut through the narrow side lanes to visit the busy staithes of the Haven. From here the visitors could see across the river Hull to the line of fortifications protecting the east bank of the river. These were built at the enormous cost of £23,000 by the order of Henry VIII and consisted of three great fortresses which were the north and south blockhouses connected to a centre castle by a huge strong wall and a moat on the other side. These solid fortresses were used as armouries, having barrels of gunpowder, cartridges and hand-grenades stored in their magazines.

The north blockhouse appeared to be badly damaged with almost a quarter of its wall blown away. Only the previous Saturday, the 16th of September, a cannoneer had entered it to fetch some cartridges for his gun with a length of lighted match in his hand! Close by were nine or ten hand-grenades which, not surprisingly, blew up and killed the soldier and four others with him. The explosion also blew the door off its hinges in the very next room, inside were stored twelve barrels of gunpowder – two of the barrels being open!

Luckily, the damaged wall was on the inside of the defences, otherwise the blockhouse would have been wide open to the enemy. Had the gunpowder also fired, the whole building would have been blown up together with the hundred men inside it, serious damage would have been caused to the adjacent town area and the enemy would have been given clear access through the blockhouse wall to swarm in and capture Hull.

During Cromwell's short visit, the evacuation of Sir Thomas' cavalry was going ahead, Lord Willoughby came over from Barton and messages were despatched to London and Kings Lynn. Now that the port of Kings Lynn was in Parliamentarian hands, communication between London and Hull was safer. The townspeople of Hull were disappointed to hear that Colonel Cromwell was not staying on with them to help fight Newcastle's army.

When he left Hull, the Humber river seemed to be alive and teeming with boats, as many as could be loaded with cavalry were crossing to Barton and returning with every tide. Moored in the river and all on full alert, many of Parliament's big ships were on constant guard stretching from the North Sea as far as the River Trent. Ships like the *Undaunted*, the *Resolution*, and the *Hercules* recently returned from London, assisted by the *Lion* and the *Employment*, were all standing-by and guarding the coastline.

Lady Anne Fairfax, accompanied by their daughter Mary, came down to the boats to wish her husband 'God Speed.' Knowing that it was not possible to travel with him this time she gave him one of her embroidered mottoes as a keepsake, as true and valiant as the lady herself the motto read 'Rather dye than truth deny.' Accompanied by many of his brave and loyal officers, Sir Thomas prepared to sail from Hull and march to join the Eastern Association army in their defence of Lincolnshire.

Getting the horses on board the boats was a tricky business and they required very careful handling. Some of the horses were skittish and eager to leave the City sensing the fresh, Lincolnshire countryside a couple of miles away. Blindfolds helped to quieten the nervous ones who were then led down the wooden planks and onto the boat's moving deck.

Reaction of the horses as they lurched about on the unsteady deck was always unpredictable. The troopers were ready for them, coaxing, yelling and guiding their mounts into positions around the mainmast, where they were securely tied and held for the duration of the crossing. On average, about a dozen of the horses with their riders and equipment could be carried across at one time, although this depended entirely upon the size of the boat waiting to be loaded.

Tides were another problem and had to be carefully judged. If the tides were too low, the horses would have to disembark onto the mud banks instead of further up in the creeks. There were accidents of course, no-one expected the operation to be without any. A boat would run aground on the mud here and there, sometimes the horses would become helplessly stuck, soldiers too, and equipment fell overboard.

The boat-owners, using their own local knowledge of the coastline, headed for the pre-arranged places but wear and tear on the creeks often forced the boats to move along the coastline looking for fresh, untrampled landing areas. When this happened, the troops waiting to escort them safely ashore had to mount and race after the boats! Protection could be random, especially if the enemy arrived while the agitated horses were being untied, quietened and led off the boats.

Evacuation of the cavalry from Hull was well under way when Cromwell arrived back in Barton on Humber, awaiting him was the heavy responsibility of delivering all these men safely back to Boston with the threat of an advancing enemy behind them.

When the last boat landed the final cargo, everyone sighed with relief, the Parliamentary troops were tired but satisfied. It had been a very busy and hazardous operation to transfer the twenty one troops of cavalry across two miles of open, fast-flowing river, and land them safely in the next county. All this in the face of the enemy. Some boats were caught by the tide turning and were swept further out into the North Sea where they sailed down the coastline, hoping to catch up with some of the bigger vessels transporting passengers and cargo down the coast to Saltfleetby Haven.

Before the march to Boston could begin all the horses had to be rounded up, some had escaped during the landings and wandered off into the marshes looking for fresh pasture. Many troops were scattered about the coastline and there was also a search for the walking stragglers whose horses had gone missing. When all were mustered and accounted for there was the business of checking and issuing equipment. Scores of Thomas Fairfax's cavalrymen who had managed to join him in Hull from the Yorkshire moors and dales, arrived in a sorry state without uniform, swords or pistols. Aware that Hull had no surplus of these items, the Earl had sent a boatload of arms for the cavalry as well as muskets and powder for use in Hull.

Now for the next hazard, could they get through to Boston safely? Cromwell was anxious to get away and urged the officers to get their men moving as soon as possible. The enemy had already hindered several landing parties, only to withdraw as soon as Cromwell's troops arrived in time to challenge them, but not for much longer, there were more Royalists on their way here.

It was a frustrating journey relentlessly pursued by the enemy who now consisted of thirty four colours of horse and dragoons. Cromwell's main priority was to deliver all his Association horse to Boston intact and ready for the Earl of Manchester's arrival there from Lynn with the Association army.

The enemy's driving ambition was to overtake Cromwell and Fairfax, then force them to stand and fight before they could slip through the fenlands to reach Boston. Once into the fens, the Parliamentarians would be on home ground and able to use the cover of trees and undergrowth in the meeres to hide in.

Thomas Fairfax found that the county of Lincolnshire was very different from his beloved Yorkshire. It was not long before he and his troops realised that combat tactics were also different here. In his own county, there were the moors, hills and dales to hide in – and to launch surprise attacks from. This part of the county was flat land dominated by a ridge of hills and whoever kept to the hills held the advantage. When the ridges gave way to flat expanses of treacherous fenlands, only the fenmen claimed advantage.

It was here that Fairfax learned more about the vagaries of knowing the enemy's whereabouts. He knew that Cromwell's own troops were from the fen areas of Ely, Bedford and Huntingdon: Willoughby had his own Lincolnshire troops and the men from Boston were quite at home in the East and West Fens. Cromwell assured him that once they left the Wolds and descended into the fenland, the Association Horse would be safer – but only if they could reach it first.

The Parliamentarians were quite aware that the Royalists, who had recently been joined by twenty fresh troops, ten companies of dragoons and about a thousand of General King's own foot, now contemptuously regarded them as 'cowardly rebels'. To a man like Fairfax, this continual hasty retreat smacked of cowardice, although as a stranger to the county he was unable to do anything other than trust his companions.

*   *   *   *   *   *

The journey to Boston was nearly at an end and the Royalists had not been sighted for some hours, when they stopped for the last night's quarter on the edge of 'Holland', the flat area of Lincolnshire around the Wash. There, on the hills about four miles from Horncastle, five of Lord Willoughby's troops were entrusted with patrolling the outposts against enemy attack, while three of Cromwell's troops took the inner guard posts.

Francis, Lord Willoughby of Parham and Lord Lieutenant of Lincolnshire, had been in charge of the county's defences until very recently – September 20th – when Lincolnshire became a part of the Eastern Counties Association. As soon as it belonged to the Association, the county was commanded by the Earl of Manchester. Possibly this affected some of their loyalty to Parliament, but by then Willoughby's command was already lacking in enthusiasm and efficiency.

Disaster very nearly struck the Association Horse. The Royalists, closing in fast during the night of the 27th September, made an early morning attack on Willoughby's outposts – who immediately raced away without attempting to give an alarm to other guards. It was sheer bad luck for the Royalists that three of Cromwell's troops, patrolling nearer to town, saw the enemy and managed to raise the alarm just in time to prevent total disaster. Several troops held the Royalists back while Cromwell and Fairfax got the army into good order and then managed to retreat into the fens. During this skirmish there were surprisingly few casualties, only about four or five, reported by each side.

The Royalists commanded by Colonel Henderson, stayed to secure the town of Horncastle by leaving all their Infantry, ten companies of Dragoons and four colours of Horse there, then with the remaining fifty troops of Horse, Henderson advanced towards Bolingbroke Castle, searching for the Association Horse.

Cromwell had left fourteen troops of horse near

10. Bolingbroke castle today — a view approaching from the south.

Bolingbroke, hoping to gain some time for his army to slip into the fens. When Colonel Henderson arrived, the fourteen troops appeared to be willing to stand and fight, then to the fury of the Royalist troops, after causing a delay they suddenly scattered and raced for the safety of the fens. Henderson's troops eventually found some of the infantry crossing a bridge near Hagnaby and attempted another attack, which again could not hold the Parliamentarians from the fens.

In disgust, and assuming that the Association cavalry had probably already got through Boston and were heading on towards Kings Lynn, Henderson returned to his garrison at Newark, to await another chance.

Colonel Cromwell's relief at bringing the Yorkshire Horse safely into Boston was soon marred by bitter disappointment. His men desperately needed their pay which had been owing to them for several weeks and their grievances were certainly not helped when Manchester had sent his own, recently paid troops, to assist Cromwell on the Hull journey.

Before leaving Boston, Cromwell had written letters asking for the money owing to his men, and so, when he opened his dispatch box on 28th September, he fully expected news that the money was waiting for him. Instead, there were plenty of letters waiting for his attention, but no authorisation for money.

Parliament was already in a desperate situation, having lost most of the north and west counties. Cromwell discovered that money was not coming in from Essex and the other counties that were left to support the Association. Weekly assessments had been levied and men impressed into the army, but the only money Cromwell had received for his men so far had come from Huntingdon. He had already used £1200 of his own private money and also borrowed money in Nottingham which Parliament still owed to him.

The Colonel had been so confident that the money would be waiting in Boston: his men had trusted him to get their pay and now he had to let them down. Manchester's men, rebellious at having to leave their own county at harvest time, were also expecting their pay – even though they were not so far in arrears as his own men.

Cromwell called his officers together and told them that there was no money for the troops. He was furious and the tears stung in his eyes as he faced the officers, knowing the reaction they would receive from the troops. He wrote letters again requesting the money and then turned to answer the rest of his correspondence. There was a complaint about one of his troop's behaviour, another complaint about a sequestered horse he was using, more petty complaints, warrants to sign and reports to write. With patience running short Cromwell answered his mail demanding that the offending troop, so diligently collecting supplies in Suffolk, should be sent to help him defend Lincolnshire. He queried the sequestered horse that he himself was using, suggesting that if wrongly taken by his men he would pay for it rather than keep the horse illegally. If Mr Goldsmith of Wilby could prove himself not to be a Royalist sympathiser, the horse or the money for it would be repaid.

After answering all his letters and writing several reports on his recent activities, there remained his visit to the Earl of Manchester in Kings Lynn.

During the latter part of their journey to Boston, Fairfax and Cromwell had discussed their situation and saw how well it fitted into their plans. The Royalists would now be very confident that their enemy was unwilling to stand and fight, a further encouragement for them to come in and undertake the defence of their threatened garrison in Bolingbroke Castle.

The two men decided that the plan should be put before the Earl of Manchester as soon as Cromwell could speak with him in Kings Lynn.

4.

Kings Lynn, A Visit to Ely
and on to Boston

'. . . until they had acquainted My Lord . . . '

O N HIS ARRIVAL IN KINGS LYNN, Cromwell went immediately to the headquarters of Edward Montagu, 2nd Earl of Manchester. The Earl was waiting for him and very anxious to hear of all that had taken place on the Hull journey.

After he had presented him with the letters from Lord Fairfax and various other Hull dignitaries, the Colonel spent some considerable time giving detailed reports regarding the enemy's strength, position and tactics. Manchester was keen to hear of the conditions inside Hull and also needed information on the Royalist regiments involved with Newcastle and the siege there. Concerned to hear about the treachery of Lord Willoughby's outpost, he decided that such a serious matter should be referred to the Council of War. When Cromwell finished his report, the proposed suggestion of luring Henderson into a trap was discussed.

Manchester listened carefully to everything that Cromwell had to tell him then, when the interview was over and Cromwell had gone to his own quarters, the Earl settled down to glance through all his dispatches. Finally, after reading the letter from Lord Fairfax once again, he sat for a while quietly speculating on the new situation. Now that the Yorkshire Horse was integrated into the Association army an assault on the enemy was a more viable proposition.

The Earl at forty-one years old was a heavy, humourless man, well-respected by the House of Lords and a devout Presbyterian. His brother Walter, to the Earl's embarrassment, was a Roman Catholic. The working relationship between Cromwell and his General was efficient rather than friendly:

some years before when they had crossed swords over a fenland drainage dispute, Cromwell had lost his temper in court with the Earl and had been ordered to make a public apology. At that time the situation between them was already difficult owing to the Earl's family having purchased Hinchingbrooke House, the beautiful home of Cromwell's impoverished uncle in Huntingdon. If Cromwell still bore a grudge, he never gave a hint, always obeying the Earl's orders in a totally disciplined and respectful manner.

As soon as Manchester was ready, all the senior officers were summoned to a meeting where the arrangements for an imminent march to Boston were finalised. The assembled leaders were then briefed by Cromwell about his knowledge of the enemy's scorn and eagerness to fight with them, thus giving rise to the belief by Sir Thomas Fairfax and himself that Henderson would easily be drawn into a trap by a suggested ruse. The excitement in the room increased quickly as all the colonels began discussing strategy and several plans were drawn up, only to be re-arranged, then corrected again, and finally studied with growing enthusiasm.

Although not a brilliant tactician in warfare, the General was a most efficient administrator. His staff were immediately able to produce lists of all his army supplies, ordnance, powder, muskets and availability of local regiments and troops. Together with his experienced and loyal officers, he felt satisfied that a successful victory was possible, and the plan was agreed upon.

When Sir William Harlackenden arrived in Kings Lynn with money from the Association's Committee at Cambridge, the payment discussions became quite overheated. Sir William, who had been actively pressing the Earl's urgent demands for more men, money, ordnance, and clothing, had only managed to bring £600 with him.

Manchester was furious, insisting that £600 was as good as nothing to them since he had already laid out further sums during the last fortnight to equip the Essex forces. The Essex new recruits had arrived in a state of wretchedness, having no coats, arms, colours or drums. After all this expenditure, there was now more than £900 owing and

Captain Rich was complaining that almost £500 was owed to him. Two thousand one hundred coats in green cloth lined with red had been ordered for Manchester's infantrymen, but Sir William was only able to confirm that two hundred were ready – unfortunately, the suppliers were holding back for their money in advance. The only good news was that the requested twenty five carriage loads of ordnance and ammunition had just arrived in Kings Lynn.

The Earl decided that if the Association army was to succeed at all he would have to take over the administration of all the county Committees himself, using his position as Major General to command more respect and power for the committeemen and their fund-raising. Sir William was ordered to accompany Manchester on his journey to Boston the next day where he would be needed to help the Earl in organising several matters.

While Cromwell was in Kings Lynn he was able to call on his brother-in-law, Valentine Walton, now appointed as the Lieutenant Governor of Lynn. Colonel Walton, from Huntingdonshire, was the husband of Margaret, Cromwell's sister, and their son Valentine was Captain of one of Cromwell's troops. The two men discussed the matters of the day and cheerfully remembered an occasion when they had seized, for Parliament, £20,000 worth of silver plate that had been on its way to the King. When the Association army moved out of Lynn to go to Boston, Walton would remain behind to guard the town with a troop of Horse and six companies of Foot.

At last, Cromwell was able to leave the town and ride home to Ely. There was business for him to attend to in the town's garrison and he was eager to see his family again.

*   *   *   *   *   *   *

Ely's distinctive cathedral had just begun to turn into a dark shadow looming over the surrounding fenland, when Cromwell and his accompanying guards finally arrived. The shadows hid years of neglect suffered by the great decaying cathedral, now in desperate need of repair with much of its lead and stained glass lost.

His house was a welcome sight after a month away from home. It was September 4th when he was last here, Harlakenden had brought him a message from Manchester and had then stayed to dine with them. As Cromwell reached the house he could see the warm glow of a hearth fire through the parlour window, its flames were making patterns flicker and dance on the panelled walls inside. Passing near to the kitchen on his way to the stables, he caught the mouth-watering smell of home-cooking.

The Rectory house in Ely had been left to Cromwell by his uncle in 1636, a fair sized brick and stone building with a tiled roof and situated right next door to the Church of St.Mary. The family home consisted of a hall, parlour, kitchen, buttery, larder, milkhouse etc., with several bedchambers above them. Adjoining the house was the massive Sextry Barn that was used for storing all the produce collected as tithes from properties in Ely. Behind the house were stables and out-houses, also a private garden well stocked with herbs, where Cromwell's two youngest daughters often played while the older children sat reading.

This welcome inheritance from his mother's brother greatly improved the quality of life for the family of Cromwell, who had been a hard-pressed farmer at St. Ives. His mother, Elizabeth, the sister of the late Sir Thomas Steward, was now 78 years old and had lived with Oliver and his family since 1617 when she had become a widow. Her brother, Sir Thomas Steward, had been a sheep farmer on a considerable scale, holding the Lordship of the Manor of Stuntney, also the lease of the Rectory of Ely with several pastures and the profits from the tithes of two parish churches, all now inherited by his nephew Oliver.

When Cromwell's wife, also called Elizabeth, heard her husband arrive she sent the boys out to help him dismount and stable his horse, called to the girls who were preparing the table for a meal, and hurried out to greet him, automatically removing her soiled apron on the way. The family were overjoyed to see him, the two smallest girls, Mary and Frances who had been born here in Ely, climbed onto his knees and almost strangled him with their hugs and kisses whilst the older girls busied around him taking care of his armour, riding boots, helmet and buff-coat.

Bridget was the oldest girl, a serious minded and religious young lady of nineteen years, then there was Elizabeth who was fourteen years old, named after, and the most like, her mother. She was quite pretty and of a totally different character to Bridget, being full of fun and quite a wilful young lady. Her father, who could refuse her nothing, called her 'Bettie' and adored her even though he often worried about her frivolous nature.

Oliver, at twenty years old, was the eldest boy since Robert had died six years ago at the age of sixteen years. A captain of a troop in his father's cavalry regiment, young Oliver was of a similar nature to Bridget and was well liked and popular with his troop. Richard, aged seventeen years was still at home with the Ely garrison, an easy-going boy who disliked serious reading and thinking, very much different to Henry, who at fifteen years old was a bright, energetic boy with a strong and intelligent character, keen to follow in his father's footsteps.

Elizabeth, Cromwell's wife, was also a striking character. She had a good sense of humour although she took her role of wife and mother very seriously. Always needing to practise full economy with a large family she took care to waste nothing and was still unused to the further improvement in their circumstances when Cromwell had recently been made Governor of the Isle of Ely. Loyal and very fond of her husband, she was not frightened of him and spoke her mind when necessary. This was a close and happy family enjoying one of their rare evenings together since the war began.

After the meal they all retired to the parlour and were entertained by Bridget and young Elizabeth who volunteered to sing some of their fathers's favourite ballads and hymns. Here with his family he gathered up the warming memories to recall on bitter nights away from home, like the haunting beauty of their clear, young voices as they sang the verses and begged him to join in with the old, melodic refrains. When the girls became tired of singing, Mary, who was six years old, and Frances aged five, drew pictures and recited for him, then nestled sleepily against their father as he relaxed in his chair listening to the excited chattering of the older children.

The conversation turned to more serious topics as the boys brought him up to date with all the local news, and a more sombre mood came over the family seated round the parlour fire. Henry was eager to hear all about the journey back from Hull and Elizabeth was concerned to hear whether Sir Thomas's wife, Lady Anne, had fully recovered from the ordeal of her capture near Bradford. Mary, the Fairfaxes' five years old daughter, had also been with them during their escape from Bradford. The frightened child was totally exhausted after twenty four hours in the saddle and had to be left behind at a farmhouse, having collapsed in her nurse's arms.

Young Bettie Cromwell was fascinated by Mary Fairfax's adventure, her relief at Mary's recovery and subsequent arrival at Barton was only matched by the thrill of hearing that Mary had a ship sent over from Hull, especially to reunite her with her family. Wide-eyed and thoughtful, the children were brought back again to face the reality of the enemy's impending approach.

A sadness invaded the room, the evening had passed too quickly and the fire quickly lost its warming glow as the ashes built up in the hearth. Before the tired family went to their beds, prayers were said for the safety of all and God's blessing was asked for Parliament, with glorious victories for its army.

The next morning, Cromwell rose early and went over to the garrison in Ely where he spent some time with Henry Ireton, whom he had appointed as his deputy governor the last August. The thirty-two year old major, single, well educated and with a natural ability for leadership was attracted to Bridget Cromwell, and both she and her parents found the attentions of this religious young man most agreeable. Ireton had been a major in Sir Francis Thornhagh's cavalry regiment when they had joined Cromwell the previous July in the fight for Gainsborough. An active Puritan, he was a cousin of John Hutchinson, the Parliamentarian Governor of Nottingham. When Sir Francis was taken prisoner at Gainsborough,

Cromwell incorporated Ireton and his troop into his own regiment, stationing him in the garrison at Ely.

Cromwell signed warrants for Ireton to collect payments for the troops and attended yet again to more letters, complaints and requests. He went home to pick up the clean clothing and freshly baked food that Elizabeth had been busy packing for him, and then said goodbye again to his elderly mother. As he kissed his wife and the tearful youngsters, the Colonel promised them that he would write home more often, then mounted his horse and rode away at the head of his escort to rejoin Manchester and Colonel Russell at Kings Lynn.

*   *   *   *   *   *   *

The size of the Association army had now swelled with the arrival in Kings Lynn of various companies and regiments summoned in from local counties. The Norfolk and Suffolk Foot regiments and cavalry arrived with their Association Colonel, Sir Miles Hobart of Plumstead, in Norfolk. Sir Miles, whose infantry were known as 'Hobart's Foote', was a Puritan and had been with Cromwell and Palgrave at the seige of Burghley House in July. Hobart had also maintained guard with his company of dragoons at Crowland and Wisbech.

At last they all began to move out of the recently captured port, marching towards Boston where the Lincolnshire regiments and Association horse were waiting for the army to join them. Through the flat, fenland country, columns of marching soldiers stretched for miles along the narrow fen roads, surrounded on either side by marshes. Through deep fords they waded and over dozens of precarious, small bridges that spanned swollen rivers and drains. A high 'spring' tide had swept down the East Coast the previous night causing havoc and flooding along the whole of the coastline, backing up the sluices, dykes and rivers for miles inland.

On towards Spalding, Pinchbeck, Surfleet and Gosberton they advanced, passing through many fen villages whose people came running out to stare and cheer at the impressive cavalcade. The Earl travelled in his coach, his own mobile quarters. Soon, the famous tower of St. Botolph's church became visible in the distance. Standing tall and dominating all the surrounding fenlands, the medieval lantern tower directed them towards the port of Boston, where in that town of confirmed loyalty to Parliament, the Association army would be welcomed and safely quartered for the next five days.

11. St. Botolph's church seen today at a distance of about three miles, from between Frampton and Wyberton, on the road that would then have been used on approaching from Kings Lynn. Although visible from at least ten miles distance only its height would have been identifiable.

5.

Boston . . . the Key of the Associated Counties . . .

SOLDIER ON WATCH DUTY at the top of St. Botolph's church tower yawned and stretched his arms. The dawn was breaking and a cockerel on the other side of the Bar Ditch began crowing. In spite of the cold and his tiredness, the soldier was fascinated by the sudden awakening of this sleepy town below him.

Soon after the cockerel's call faded away a gate latch clapped somewhere down in Wormgate and footsteps resounded on the cobblestones; a baby cried in one of the nearby houses and a woman's voice rang out loudly as she began calling her family to wake up and rise. There were sounds of activity all around him as doors banged shut, pans clattered, dogs began barking, and a man called out a greeting to his neighbour as they passed each other. Waking children added their own fretful voices to the rapidly increasing hubbub.

The dark rooftop shapes began to take on a clearer pattern in the early light. Wisps of wood smoke crawled out of the closely jumbled chimneys, dipped and curled lethargically around the roofs before the early morning breezes snatched up the vapours and carried them up into the air and away from the town.

The river below him was changed from a black ribbon of the night-time into an urgently moving reality. Leaning out as far as he dared, he could see some of the fishing boats moored below the church. Further down the river near the Packhouse Quay he could see some prisoners, in chains and guarded by soldiers: they were being taken across to a ship in the river waiting to convey them to London. From the cells of the

Guildhall opposite the quay, many of the political prisoners were dispatched by sea to stand trial in London.

Gradually, the early clatter of the sleepy town grew louder until it strengthened into a bustling din. Boston was fully awake again and it was Monday the 9th of October, the start of another busy day – and busier than usual for some of its occupants!

The inns alongside the river seemed very quiet that morning compared with the noise of the singing, laughing and shouting of last night. All around the town centre, Parliamentarian officers were quartered in local hostelries such as the Red Lion, the Falcon, the Peacock, Three Tuns and many others. There was quite an abundance of inns in the town, a legacy from the busy medieval days, and recently the majority of them had usually been crowded at night with soldiers. Bostonians had become accustomed to the regular sight of officers and men of the watch escorting drummers through the streets to beat the evening tattoo. This custom was a signal for the publican to turn off his ale taps, refuse all his military clients any more drink, and then send them back to their camp.

Somewhere below him, another soldier called up to the sentry who turned away from the parapet, grateful that his cold night watch was over at last. Descending the 365 stone steps, his musket and sword clanged noisily behind him against the confining stone walls of the tower.

Downstairs in the church, which was large and tailor-made for such an emergency, there were troopers checking through a mass of stored equipment ready and waiting to be loaded onto the waggons. Groups of horse-boys were busy feeding and grooming horses that belonged to the commanding officers. These valuable horses were usually to be found tethered to the pillars and walls inside the largest and the driest buildings in the town, strong, well-built places that offered security and a look-out tower above them – the churches.

At the eastern end of the church the exquisitely carved choir stalls were piled high with swords, pistols, pieces of armour, saddles and bridles. Two old vestries that remained from the days of the medieval Guilds served as temporary offices and in one of them an officer was assisting the Provost Marshall who carried a staff or truncheon as a sign of his authority. His duties were to keep a check on provisions – a sort of weights and measures man – and to lay hands on him would result in the death penalty; accompanying him was an auditor who was confirming the prices of victuals.

12a. A view of the interior of St. Botolph's church, Boston, where many of Cromwell's men were quartered a few days prior to the Battle of Winceby. This photograph of the modern interior gives some idea of the space available for the troops and horses and shows some of the twelve pillars used as tethering posts. The Victorian box pews now in the nave did not then occupy the floor space.

12b. The lower illustration shows some of the choir stalls which were then (and still are) present and used for depositing the arms and armour.

At the foot of the stairs leading to the new library, two guards were in earnest conversation with their captain, and nearby were trumpeters and drummers preparing to leave, some waiting impatiently for their orders. Inside a very old corner chapel and propped against the walls were dozens of the army's standards and colours or guidons, all with their precious silken colours neatly furled and under heavy guard until the standard-bearers and cornets collected them. Outside the great double oak doors in the south porch, a group of local boys were excitedly approaching the soldiers guarding the doorway. The presence of the army in the town had exhilarated many of the youngsters who jostled with each other as they begged favours. A couple of the boys who had just been allocated some menial tasks turned with triumphant grins to leer at their less favoured companions.

There was plenty to do for the greater part of the army was moving out of Boston that day, several troops of cavalry had already left on local scouting duties. The church had to be cleaned, the straw burnt, and all the equipment and stores had to be packed into waggons or loaded on carts. Local owners of horses and carts were hired to supply straw and feed for the cavalry mounts and then transport it to Bolingbroke, others carried locally baked bead, ale, or powder and match for the musketeers.

Time passed, and the town seemed to vibrate to the sound of drummers constantly sounding the several beats which called the soldiers to their Ensigns, to assemble at the rendez-vous, or to begin marching. All the surrounding infantry regiments were mustering ready for the march northwards to Bolingbroke Castle.

The din was tremendous, and could be heard for miles around. The louder the drums beat, the louder the watching townspeople had to shout to each other as farewell messages were relayed to and from the soldiers. Somewhere in the crowd inconsolable babies screamed with fright. Excited dogs raced about barking hysterically amongst a group of young children who strutted up and down waving their wooden sticks for make-believe muskets and pikes, mimicking the postures of the soldiers.

*　　*　　*　　*　　*　　*　　*

Boston people were well used to sharing the town with the military, and as long as they belonged to Parliament there was no problem. Certainly in the last few days, the town had been filled to bursting with soldiers since the Association army had arrived here, but they were leaving now to attack Bolingbroke castle and chase the Royalists out of Lincolnshire. Everyone was predicting success, feeling happy to see such a large force back to protect the Holland County area. News had just reached them that the Royalists had recently deserted their garrison at Wainfleet, leaving only the castle at Bolingbroke as a main target.

The officers were still shouting orders and, in turn, the sergeants bellowing even louder when the Earl of Manchester's coach arrived. Shortly after he stepped down from his carriage, the Earl was greeted by Lord Willoughby of Parham and other gentlemen, including the aldermen and councillors of Boston, Thomas Coney the Town Clerk, Richard Westland the mayor, and the vicar of Boston, the Rev. Anthony Tuckney. High hopes went with the official send-off.

As the last of the baggage carts rumbled away behind the army, the drumbeats had already begun to fade away into the distance. A hushed anxiety seemed to settle over Boston as groups of worried townfolk stood around in the deserted streets, they were talking quietly and looking northwards. It was going to be difficult to settle down again after the upheaval of the last few days.

Some of the local girls were in tears after the recent partings with their sweethearts and tried to comfort each other as they walked back to their homes.

The main topic of conversation amongst the men concerned the army of the Eastern Association and whether it had the ability to check the Royalist advance into Lincolnshire. If not, there was a great deal of reckoning to be done, the enemy would make life especially grim for the inhabitants of Boston.

The marshy fens had been an important means of survival for the commoners until King Charles sent the Dutchmen in to drain these fens, leaving many of the villagers destitute. Small armies of angry, desperate men had fallen upon the new drains, banks and hedges, demolishing them as fast as they

13. These photographs were taken just north of New Bolingbroke to either side of the main Boston to Horncastle road (B1183) some nine miles north of Boston in the West Fen area when there had been no particularly heavy rainfall in the preceding month. Despite modern drainage facilities even now the land can easily become waterlogged.

were built. So very widespread was the defiance that little had been able to be done to curb it, orders issued by the House of Lords were mostly contemptously ignored, whilst Parliament, anxious not to offend the people, warily advised against violence.

During 1642, the sheriff of Lincolnshire had vainly attempted to restore order in the county. In April, a crowd of three hundred local people smashed dykes, destroyed crops and pulled down some houses at Bolingbroke: they laughed at the sheriff and J.Ps., defiantly disobeying all their orders. When some of the rioters were arrested and taken to Boston, a huge crowd of more than a thousand arrived to rescue the prisoners. Yes, retribution would surely be heaped upon the heads of all the Fen people for their rebellious actions, if the Royalists came.

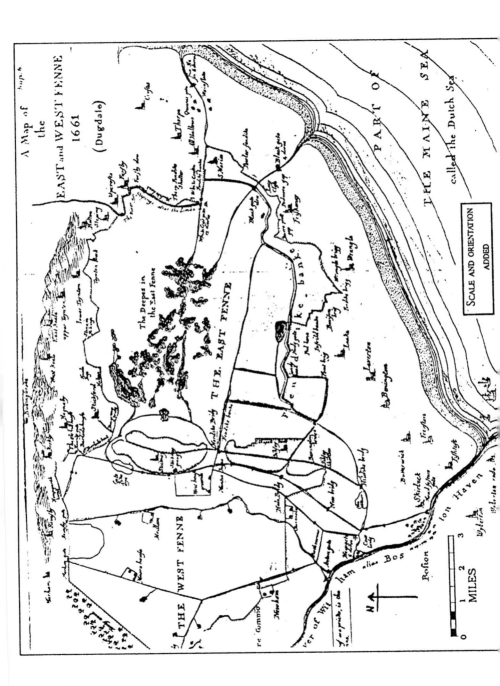

52.

6.

NORTHDYKE CAUSEWAY, STICKNEY AND BOLINGBROKE
'. . . mud and meeres, words and castles . . .'

ᴬDVANCING NORTHWARDS in a seemingly endless column, the Association army moved slowly along the Northdyke causeway, a wide stretch of stony ground raised well above vast areas of flooded land and separating the East and West fens. Beside the marshes, tall willow trees flourished so well that they needed cutting back regularly in order to prevent the highway from becoming overgrown and impassable for coaches.

On the right-hand side was the East fen, a vast overgrown area of meeres and marsh giving off a steaming, fetid mist. By comparison the West fen was totally different, almost bare except for the canals left by the Dutch engineers in their attempts to drain the land.

Even though the busy carriage-way was constantly repaired with soil, gravel, and large stones, dozens of holes quickly reappeared when rain turned the top crust into a mudtrack. The sudden concentration of an army with its men and horses continually trampling over the muddy surface, rapidly caused severe damage and the journey soon became hazardous. Deep pot-holes in the causeway created worry and chaos for the ordnance and the baggage train handlers.

Always in a hurry to keep on the move and remain close behind the infantry, they struggled desperately to avoid the pot-holes which threatened to overturn the heavy-laden waggons. The tired men wrestled with heavy carts whose wheels were set on sliding out of control acros the slippery road, their loads tipping out as they crashed into the marshes. Spitting and cursing, the men dealt with the spate of broken shafts and wheels that usually followed these accidents, causing even further delays.

The horse boys followed on behind the baggage, bringing with them the strings of spare cavalry horses: carefully picking their way through the mud they churned it over and over again, leaving a quagmire in their wake. In the rear, and now trailing far behind the army column, the same problems were making life even more miserable for the camp-followers. This group consisted mainly of the homeless wives, mothers, sweethearts and widows of soldiers; those whose only hope of support for themselves and their children came from the army pay. The women were not all whores, many of them earned their keep in other ways such as cooking, mending, and cleaning armour, jobs that were still necessary, even in camp. On the battlefields, wounded soldiers needed attention and their dead had to be lifted and carried away on the carts by these women. The older children helped as well, trundling the carts forward to where they were needed, bringing up supplies of gunpowder and then collecting up any muskets dropped by the dead soldiers.

Trying to keep up with the army, the tired women pushed and tugged at their carts presently laden with babies and small, dirty children lying amongst the bundles of clothing and meagre personal possessions. The army was now so far ahead that the women were on their own. Up to their ankles in, and

15. A photograph taken (cf. Fig. 13.) from the A16, or approximately the Northdyke Causeway, about a mile south of Stickney looking into the East Fen also showing how easily, even today, water can still lie on the low ground (and south of Stickney all the ground is low).

54.

with clothing made heavy by the weight of, the filthy mud, they stopped to help each other haul their carts out of the mire, rescue what they could, and then trudge wearily on again.

Soon after the leading regiments had negotiated the crossing over the Nordyke bridge, they arrived in Stickney, a village built on the causeway itself. Neat and sturdy with thatched roofs, many of the mud and stud houses were arranged on each side of the roadway, their front doors opening onto the road itself. The centre of the village was crowded with groups of people standing around to see the arrival of such an army, only to be quickly dispersed when an advance group arrived to arrange quarters for the men and horses.

After only a short break in the village, ten companies of the Foot escorted by some cavalry troops, continued with the march towards Bolingbroke where they hoped to take the castle from the Royalists and secure the garrison in readiness for Manchester's arrival. Meanwhile, in Stickney, the remaining soldiers made barricades across all the possible exits and entrances into the village by using their waggons and carts to block them. The same procedure was carried out a couple of miles further on at Stickford. Guards were immediately posted on look-out duty at the top of the church tower, together with a sentry at the bottom of the tower in case there was a sudden need to shout down to him and raise the alarm quickly.

Accommodation was arranged for the cavalry in and all around the area, the largest houses were chosen first and then the smaller buildings until sufficient beds and stables for the military were found. On the opposite side of the road to the church and the vicarage was an old inn, a square, mud and stud building, its roof also well thatched with rushes gathered from the fens and having a central chimney that boasted of an open hearth down below, with a roaring fire to welcome cold, damp travellers.

The Officers who found themselves billeted at the inn were in luck, for the beds had good mattresses, all comfortably stuffed with feathers plucked from the local geese and ducks which, roasted and looking succulent, formed a part of the mouth-watering fare cooked below in the kitchen. The Rose

16. The site of the former Rose and Crown inn. The cottage by the road sign bears a plaque showing its name to be 'Rose and Crown cottage'.

and Crown was always a very popular inn, offering a welcome night's rest for all the tired wayfarers who needed to break their long journeys through Lincolnshire. Noted for its wholesome food and excellent cooking, the inn could provide a great variety of fish dishes steeped in garnishing sauces, or perhaps a baked, juicy pig covered in a crispy coat might be served up, piping hot, on the table. There was game pie, or various strong broths containing faggots of rabbit or fowl with sweet herbs and vegetables that simmered together in great pans on the hearth. Later, pear pie might follow, or pippins baked in a coffin of pastry, quinces in sweet syrup or cheese cakes containing a pound of butter and sixteen eggs! Beer and wines, especially the strong, white Spanish sack, were drinks favoured by the travellers for washing the meal down.

Shortly after the Association army arrived in Stickney, cavalry scouts were despatched to visit the north and western areas for signs of the enemy's approach. News of the Earl's intended march to capture the Bolingbroke garrison had already been allowed to leak out to the enemy, three days earlier, on the preceeding Friday. Royalist raiding parties from Newark and foraging troops from the castle at Old Bolingbroke had been a source of aggravation for the fen villagers recently, all of the troops taking supplies without attempting to pay for them. The arrival of Manchester's army was greeted with relief by the villagers as soon it was made known to them that payment warrants would be issued for supplies and quarter.

Manchester was using Stickney vicarage as his headquarters and it was here where the small groups of Parliamentary scouts regularly arrived, their horses sweating and lathered with dirt as they brought news in from the outposts. The riders often returned with their clothing and horses caked in the foul smelling mud after mislaying the fen paths and floundering about, sometimes up to their necks, in the marshes as they searched for the firmer ground again.

News arrived from Hull for the Earl of Manchester and brought him a warning that the Royalists were tightening up on the siege there, building fortifications so close to the city that musket balls could be heard flying over the walls. Starting from a new and stronger fort on the side of the Humber near Gallows Clow, the enemy's latest earth works had slanted sharply towards to the western walls of Hull where they had positioned six guns. The messenger cheerfully described how the Hull defenders had sallied out from the city, forced the Royalists to retreat and then captured the ordnance – so sparing the Royalists the trouble of carrying them back again! He confirmed that Sir John Meldrum was now in Hull with the extra soldiers, together with a further 250 men sent by Sir William Constable.

From one of the stables close to Grange House there came roars of laughter and shouts of encouragement, a group of local lads had just challenged some of the horse boys to take part in a game of quoits. It was a a lively contest and had drawn quite a crowd into the stable-yard where they stood and watched the contestants throwing. Horseshoes were used as quoits, and each time the hob was ringed two points were scored and a loud cheer went up.

Obadiah Howe, the Presbyterian rector of Stickney, was in his element playing host to the Earl of Manchester, commander of the Eastern Association army, who was also accompanied by some of his most senior officers. Panic threatened to erupt in the vicarage kitchen where his young wife, Elizabeth, was combining her domestic and hostess duties with a demented fervour. Howe was a well-educated young man of twenty-seven years, having left Magdalen Hall, Oxford, with an M.A. degree in 1638. Obadiah seemed well qualified for a promising career in the church. His father, William Howe, was the minister of nearby Tattershall.

During dinner, the conversation ranged from politics and war to life in the Fens. The rector was able to describe to his visitors some of the mixed fortunes of the local people who lived in these surrounding villages. Compared with an army life of always needing to forage in search of food, the local people, now that they had their fens back, appeared to live in a land of plenty.

The East Fen was a wild area of waterlogged land composed of many shallow lakes connected to each other by reedy marshes. The lakes were full of fish such as perch, pike, eels, bream and tench, while over in the West Fen, water fowl bred quite freely in the more open sections. There were ancient salt beds nearby of immense value for preserving food for leaner times. Some grazing land was available for the curly-coated pigs and the Lincolnshire sheep, large and well endowed with their thick, long wool. The numerous willow trees provided supple branches for roofing material, while reed cutting and peat digging were other useful sources of livelihood gained from this damp, unhealthy area.

Unfortunately, as the rector explained, there was a variety of widespread illnesses directly caused by the local conditions, old and young alike suffered from various ailments and severe debilities such as aches and pains in the joints, bronchial complaints and also a nasty malarial fever called the 'fen ague'.

While the Association commanders were being most comfortably entertained by the rector of Stickney, four miles away in the village of Bolingbroke, the siege of the Royalists in the castle had begun. Sir Miles Hobart's Foot, which was led by his Major Knight, were part of the ten companies of Association infantry that had been despatched to Bolingbroke.

Marching into the village they immediately surrounded the Castle and Major Knight opened the proceedings by sending his drummer up to the gate-house with a message, summoning the Royalist occupants of the Castle to surrender.

17. The present-day remains of Bolingbroke Castle (excavated in the 1960s) seen across the moat from the south.

18. How effectively the church tower did overlook the castle is emphasised by this view taken from within the walls.

Although the enemy managed to show some respect for the drummer and his duties, there was no doubt about the defiance in their reply. Almost as expected, the gist of the answer was that his *bugge-bear words could not win castles or make them quit the place!'*

The village and castle were both situated in an unusual position, at the bottom of Sow Dale which was a hollow in the

Wold hills, and so it was neccesary for the siege positions to be taken up along the surrounding, higher ground overlooking the enemy. Some of the highest hills like the ones called Horncastle Hill, Kirkby Hill, and Dewy Hill gave ample room for the army to camp on and maintain a clear view for keeping watch over a wide area.

The medieval castle was completely encircled by a deep, wide moat and so full of water that it managed to overflow the banks in several places. On the far side of the moat the castle had five horseshoe-shaped towers connected by a walled enclosure, the stonework bases of which were all stained green from centuries of contact with the water in the moat. Facing due north, and guarding the bridge over the moat, was a double-towered gate-house that also led into the main accomodation, the great hall and other buildings around the courtyard.

Major Knight took stock of the situation as he rode around the area, noticing that the church was very close to the castle, and that it also had a tower, which conveniently overlooked the castle walls! One of the mortar pieces could be hauled up onto the top of the church tower and be positioned high enough to fire across at the castle. He detailed some of his soldiers to go in and possess a little house on the right-hand side, between the church and the castle. After dark, they would break open the church doors, mount the mortar upon the tower and fire across into the castle itself.

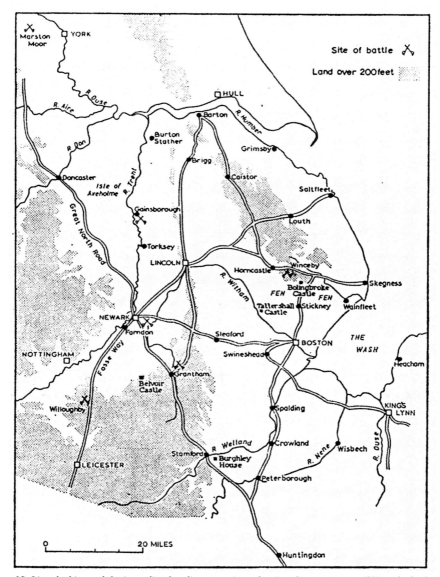

19. Lincolnshire and the immediately adjacent regions showing the orientation of Winceby both to Bolingbroke Castle and Horncastle and in the wider context of the whole area in the Civil War.

61.

7.

Tuesday morning Oct 10th 1643

BOLINGBROKE, HORNCASTLE, EDLINGTON AND THIMBLEBY

' . . . some of our Horse put to run a great hazard . . . '

 UESDAY MORNING DAWNED VERY SLOWLY. Although it was clear and bright on the tops of the hills a thick blanket of grey mist covered all the low lying hollows. Coaxed out of the damp earth by a brief spell of autumn sunshine, the fog had remained dormant all night, waiting for the daylight to come again.

When dawn came the guards on the hills overlooking Bolingbroke were still unable to see down through the wet, grey shadows into the village, only the faint shapes of the castle towers were visible to them. Nearby, on all the highest slopes of the hills surrounding the little village, lay the make-shift tents and campfires of Parliamentarian soldiers. In the damp morning air, wood-smoke from dozens of fires hovered around the soldiers as, bleary-eyed and shivering, the men swung their arms and stamped their feet to warm up, coughing and spitting as they inhaled the acrid smoke.

Barricades had been built across all the local footpaths and roads cutting the village off altogether, the guards allowing no-one to enter or leave without a written pass. Inside the castle, the besieged Royalists were eager and ready for some live target practice. Watching and listening, they laid in wait behind the walls of the gate-house and castle towers for the first signs of enemy movement near the village.

After making their way on horseback through the narrow Bolingbroke lanes, Major Knight and Quartermaster-General Vermuyden approached the church and then dismounted, keeping cover behind a nearby cottage as they inspected the damage caused to the church during the night. Major Knight's plans to mount the mortar on top of the church tower the previous night had met with disaster, the noise his men created as they attempted to break in during the night had alerted the Royalists who, guessing what the Parliamentarians were about, fired across at the church tower, setting its thatch ablaze and illuminating the whole operation.

As soon as the two officers moved forward to view the line of fire, there was a sudden hail of musket shot from the castle and several of their escorting soldiers fell wounded or dead. The Quartermaster gasped and limped away to take cover, muttering oaths in his own Dutch tongue as he went. Thanks to his good, leather riding boots, the shot that hit Vermuyden's ankle did not pierce the skin but merely left him bruised and limping. The Royalist musketeers on the Castle ramparts began laughing and jeering, still shouting defiance and confidently forcasting that their Colonel Henderson would soon be arriving with his army to rout and chase the enemy back into the fens again.

Meanwhile, the Earl of Manchester and Colonel Cromwell were preparing to leave Stickney vicarage and rendezvous with other senior officers at Kirkby, one mile outside Bolingbroke. It was arranged that Manchester should leave three of his own companies behind, as a rearguard protection in case of a necessary retreat to Boston.

Five miles west of Bolingbroke, Sir Thomas Fairfax was quartered in Horncastle. Several troops of cavalry were quartered in villages to the north of Horncastle and as far south as the bridge over the river Witham at Tattershall, all forming a watching shield of outguards along the westerly approaches to Horncastle. Between these outguards and the town of Horncastle, more troops of the Association horse were deployed as an inner, widespread barrier of mobile sentinels, ready and waiting to despatch an immediate early warning to Fairfax as soon as the Royalist advance was sighted. He, in turn, would relay the alarm back to the Earl of Manchester at his quarters at Kirkby. News that Henderson was on the way with his Royalist army had already reached them, but where was he? To discover the size and whereabouts of Henderson's army was of vital importance and Manchester was impatiently waiting for them to bring him this information.

Many of the Yorkshire troops were riding in unfamiliar countryside as they patrolled the approaches from Lincoln, Gainsborough and Newark, watching for a sighting of the Royalists. With loaded pistols, a trumpeter ready to sound the alarm, and the pass-word of 'Religion' given to all Parliamentary troops, the various outposts rode back and forth amongst villages, in and out of woods, checking bridges across rivers, peering all the time through the mists that swirled below them in the valleys. As the morning passed, still with no sighting of the enemy, tension mounted amongst the troopers and imagination began to play its tricks upon the edgy men.

In these circumstances it was easy for some to go too far afield and lose the way back to their quarters. Two troops of horse, who were quartered only two miles outside Horncastle, at Thimbleby, soon realised how far off course they had strayed when the landmark of Lincoln Cathedral loomed much larger and nearer to them than at their last sighting of it. The two captains, Moody and Player, immediately ordered a rapid about-turn and hurried away, hoping to find their way back to quarters again. Disaster was waiting for them. A detachment of one thousand Royalist cavalrymen had infiltrated the area during their absence and were moving steadily towards Horncastle – where Fairfax was waiting for his outposts to bring him an advance warning.

Obviously out-numbered, the two captains of the returning troops gloomily surveyed the enemy from a distance and then decided that there was only one course of action left to them – that was to brazen it out and try to get through to Horncastle and alert Fairfax. Captain Samuel Moody of Hobart's cavalry and Captain Player, of Fairfax's, agreed upon a daring and courageous plan, they would attack the enemy, making a tremendous noise as if they were the Forlorn Hope charge of a large army. By delaying the discharging of their pistols until they were very close to their targets, the shots would be more deadly and the impact might be sufficient to help the two troops to fight their way through. Courage and resolve saw them through the enemy lines. There were casualties of course, on both sides, but on the whole the plan worked well for them.

*   *   *   *   *   *   *

At Edlington, three miles further north, Captain Johnson was also returning with his troop after spending most of the day searching for the enemy. Pockets of mist were gathering again and enveloping the low-lying areas when Johnson, a captain in Hobart's cavalry, decided to move up onto the clearer, higher ground where his men would be safer. Suddenly, ahead of him in the mist, he noticed horses grazing, campfires, soldiers and Royalist colours. At last, they had found some of the enemy's quarters.

Johnson was a competent Norfolk soldier. Last year, he and forty of his 'Yarmouth Volunteers' acting as bailiffs for the town, had disarmed and seized a ship from Holland containing one hundred and forty officers and soldiers on their way to join the King. A valuable cargo of three hundred barrels of gunpowder was siezed, as well as a bag of letters that included one with important information from Queen Henrietta to the Marquis of Newcastle. Captain Johnson and his Volunteers had been duly commended by the House of Commons for 'the great good service done to the Commonwealth'.

Stealthily, Johnson and his troop watched and waited for the right moment, then from out of the mist they attacked the camp, charging in with blood-curdling threats of vengeance and swords flashing. Taken by surprise, the Royalists were completely dispersed and Johnson was able to bring his men off without any casualties. During the fighting they had managed to capture a dozen prisoners and now had serious news for Fairfax – five thousand Royalists were verging upon Horncastle, intending to arrive before nightfall.

How this enemy unit had managed to pass, unnoticed, through the outguard posts caused Johnson a great deal of concern. If he and his troops had accidentally caught up with one small portion of the enemy who were already so close to Horncastle, why had no alarm been raised yet, and where were the rest of the five thousand Royalists?

Urging his men to use extra vigilance as they hurried towards Horncastle, Captain Johnson took his troop safely into the town, alerting all the sentries as he passed, and headed straight for Fairfax's quarters.

8.

KIRKBY AND HORNCASTLE

'. . . the best laid plans . . .'

LONG BEFORE CAPTAINS MOODY AND PLAYER encountered the enemy, Thomas Fairfax had received the news of an alarm given to one of his outpost quarters. Unfortunately, no-one seemed to be sure where the alarm had come from. With dozens of troops scouting the area between Lincoln and Tattershall watching the roads and crossing places over the river Witham, they were all on the move.

After despatching a party of horse to try and discover the source of the alarm, Fairfax sent a letter to Kirkby reporting that an alarm had been received and assuring the Earl of further news as soon as the search party returned. The waiting was an anxious time for the men in Horncastle who understood that the safety of the whole Eastern Association army relied upon their vigilance. An hour of preparation followed, extra guards and look-outs were sited on the church and tallest buildings, barriers were strengthened, while some of the people who dwelt on the western outskirts of the town constructed yet another defence barricade for their own protection.

Eventually the scouting party arrived back in Horncastle only to report that they had found no evidence of Royalist troops in the area and could only assume that the alarm must have been a mistake. Fairfax was now in a quandary, should he remain in Horncastle until dusk or should he return to Kirkby? Deciding to wait for a while, he sent another letter to the Earl informing him of events and then, with no further information of Royalist armies gathering in the area, Fairfax deemed it safe to leave Horncastle. Unaware that Captain Johnson's troop was triumphantly returning to Horncastle with prisoners and important news, he departed for Kirkby to consult with the Earl.

*   *   *   *   *   *

Near Thimbleby, the two captains, Moody and Player, were busy rounding up their own men after the recent charge through Royalist troops. Wounds were bandaged, all pistols were reloaded and the journey was quickly resumed, whereupon they immediately caught up with yet another enemy unit on the outskirts of the village. Forced once more into a similar situation, the two troops repeated their 'Forlorn Hope' attack and charged into the enemy ranks. Waving their pistols and firing as closely as possible at anyone in their way, the troops then drew their swords and began to hack their way out.

Samuel Moody looked behind him to check on how many of his men had got through and swore when he saw that his Cornet, surrounded by enemy swords, was fighting for his life while refusing to release the colours he was bearing. Seconds later the cornet toppled from his horse and lay lifeless as Moody's colours were immediately snatched up and waved triumphantly after him. Moody could feel no elation as they reached the outer barricades of Horncastle. He had lost his colours, a stigma that only the capture of an enemy colour would remove, but worse than that he had lost a good, brave officer and one who had proved worthy of his rank and trust.

Shouting a warning and still brandishing their swords, the two troops headed towards the outer barricades of Horncastle, confident that their guards would move one of the carts aside and allow them through to safety. It was quite the last straw for them when the defenders, assuming that Moody and Player's men were part of the now expected Royalist attack, delayed the two troops by fiercely resisting their attempts to re-enter the town.

*   *   *   *   *   *

As soon as the Earl of Manchester arrived at his quarters

in Kirkby, he sent word for his senior officers to join him in urgent talks. Sir Miles Hobart, Lord Willoughby of Parham and Colonel Vermuyden were amongst those who were waiting in Kirkby when he and Colonels Cromwell and Russell arrived from Stickney. The discussions naturally included Bolingbroke castle, and their chagrin that it still remained occupied and controlled by the defiant Royalists. This had now become a serious setback to their plans for it meant that any movement of Association regiments at present camped out of range on the surrounding hillsides, was dangerously restricted. They must find better quarters for the army before Henderson arrived.

There was some more news from Hull for them to talk about. The Royalists were using two demi-cannon in their attack on the city defences, one firing from the siegeworks placed between Sculscotte and Hull, the other from between Hessle and Hull. Shot weighing 35lbs had missed the high church but other shots were causing some concern amongst the defenders and so Lord Fairfax had agreed to make another attack on the Royalists. The report went on to say that five hundred soldiers and townsmen cheerfully sallied out from the city once more, attacked the nearest defences and demolished three of the works.

A coded message told them that another sally was planned to take place on the morning of Monday, October 9th, and Lord Fairfax would send news to the Earl of Manchester of the outcome. The officers at Kirkby were now waiting for the arrival of two different messengers, one from Hull and the other from Horncastle.

When the first letter from Sir Thomas Fairfax reached Kirkby headquarters, bringing them the warning of a possible alarm near Horncastle, their satisfaction in knowing that the Royalists were nearer soon became mixed with tension as the Association officers continued to wait for more details. An hour later the second letter arrived from Sir Thomas informing them that his troops had reported finding no trace of the Royalist army in the vicinity and had assumed the previous alarm to have been a mistake.

This was the deciding factor that prompted the Earl into moving his army. He and his officers had already agreed the town of Horncastle would be a more strategic place to wait for the enemy, the area surrounding it was better suited for fighting a battle than in the cramped, muddy Bolingbroke. Horncastle was only six miles away – and if they moved quickly enough there was still time to settle in.

The decision was made and messengers with new orders were immediately despatched to all the Association cavalry outposts telling them to meet the Earl in Horncastle, which was now the new 'alarm place', or rendezvous. It was arranged that the infantry would move out of Bolingbroke, leaving enough men to maintain the siege there, and join the Earl on the following morning. Committed to this change of plan, the Earl and his cavalry left Kirkby and headed north west travelling via Kirkby Hill and Horncastle Hill in order to avoid Bolingbroke and the muddy quagmire around it. The steep ascent that led them onto the Wolds was soon accomplished.

20. High ground just north-west of Bolingbroke (Kirkby Hill): probably one of the sites used for camping by the Parliamentary troops. Just below this skyline might well have been part of the Earl of Manchester's route before meeting Sir Thomas Fairfax at Scrafield.

Here, where the tiny villages of Hareby, Asgarby and Winceby used stones from the local gravel pit to maintain their footpaths and lanes, the cavalry took full advantage of the firmer ground in order to detour badly flooded areas.

Sir Thomas Fairfax, who was riding back to Kirkby, suddenly encountered the Earl just as the cavalry reached Scrafield and was about to begin the descent to Horncastle. It was an ideal place to halt. Using the shelter of the woods, the officers were able to survey the land around them and keep a watch on the road as it approached them from Horncastle. In the distance a troop of cavalry was racing towards them, obviously in a desperate haste to reach Fairfax and give him some important news.

Captain Johnson came galloping ahead of his troop, shouting a warning that the enemy had overtaken some of the outposts and then, after dismounting from his weary horse, gave the officers a full account of the incident at Edlington. The Earl listened as Johnson told him of their skirmish with the enemy and divulged the information gleaned from the prisoners who had been captured. According to Johnson's captives there were five thousand Royalists riding towards Horncastle and expected to arrive there very soon. With only his present numbers to rely upon, the Earl knew that an open encounter with five thousand Royalists was quite out of the question.

Serious news indeed, but he still hoped to occupy the town first. His cavalry reinforcements should all be on their way now to the new 'alarm place' and that would enable him to force the enemy into quartering outside the town and in the open countryside for the night. Tomorrow his infantry would join him from Bolingbroke.

Hurrying downhill towards Horncastle, the Earl's small force had almost reached the outskirts of the town when they were brought to a sudden halt by the sound of fighting inside the town. It was a great commotion made up of musket fire, the shouting and screaming of men as they fought each other, sounds of barricades being overturned and then, as the troops listened with dismay, shouts of jubilation filled the air. It seemed that Henderson had beaten them to it after all and the Royalists were now in triumphant possession of the town.

As the Parliamentarians turned and made their way back

up the hill, some of their own cavalry raced break-neck out of Horncastle after them, not as the Earl thought, his troops being beaten out of the town but Captains Moody and Player whose men had just battled their way through the town barricades with such a tremendous noise. This was the commotion that they had supposed to be the enemy taking the town.

It was now too late for the Earl to try and occupy Horncastle. The Royalists were immediately behind Moody and Player's troops and would be surging into the town at any moment. Disappointed and angry, the Earl of Manchester gave orders for his troops to retreat up the hill and return to Bolingbroke. Because of the outposts' negligence, the enemy had been able to fall upon Association quarters and then capture Horncastle, all without any warning from the look-outs who were especially posted for this purpose. Worse still, the Earl had already arranged for all his outlying troops to leave their quarters and join him in a town which was now occupied by the enemy.

For the second time that afternoon he had to change the alarm place, sending out new, urgent messages for all the outpost troops to meet him on Kirkby Hill. The Earl decided that early tomorrow, Wednesday, he would evacuate all his Association army from Bolingbroke and place them on the hills confronting Horncastle. There they would wait for the Royalists to arrive.

Relaxing slightly, the Earl demanded to know more about the Moody-Player business, he was intrigued by all the noise that the two troops had made and very concerned to see that Captain Moody had no colours with him when he arrived. Sir Miles Hobart gave him an account of the troops' escapades and their brave attempt to bring a warning to Horncastle which resulted in the loss of Captain Moody's colours.

It was agreed by all, that the enemy could hardly brag too much of this day's work, especially as all their losses were caused by so few attackers.

9.

KIRKBY HILL AND WINCEBY

' . . . left the hill and came to equal ground . . . '

HAT NIGHT, THE EARL OF MANCHESTER continued to draw the army together on the western hills above Bolingbroke. His troops abandoned all their outposts near Horncastle and came to him at the alarm place, where the muster produced an army of almost 5,000 men. As soon as a troop arrived there, the captain reported immediately to his colonel with details of any incidents during the journey. Several of them had missed the second change of orders and already made their way to Horncastle – only realising that the Royalists were already there when the password of 'Religion' created an instant hostility. Royalist guards, expecting to hear their own password of 'Cavendish', quickly gave the alarm as the bemused Association troops turned and fled back into the darkness!

Manchester's guards were positioned at all intersections leading into the area and no-one was allowed access to Kirkby Hill or its steeper neighbour, Horncastle Hill, without his permission. From dusk onwards, hundreds of campfires illuminated the higher ground and wooded areas where the army were quartered. The once peaceful countryside was totally dominated by the presence of this vast military gathering. Groups of soldiers huddled around the fires quietly discussing the day's events, some related news received from families at home and read letters aloud for the benefit of those who could not read. Others carried on lively arguments or played cards by the firelight. Singing was a popular relaxation with a variety of lyrics and vocal skills capable of entertaining all tastes. Sentimental ballads, hymns and madrigals were often interspaced by tavern choruses, bawdy songs or ditties, while occasionally, the sound of a tenor voice singing a favourite love-song would create a change of mood. When it was time for sleeping, each hillside fell silent and darker as the fires burnt low.

*   *   *   *   *   *

The Earl of Manchester remained on the hilltop all that night with his army. Sheltered from the wind by a great tent displaying his standard of figured, green damask, embossed with the words 'Truth & Peace', he conferred with members of staff, consulted rough maps, and dictated letters. His personal guard were on duty all around him, only those in authority or bearing urgent news were admitted. One of these was the messenger from Hull who had arrived tired and hungry after a journey from Barton normally lasting two, or perhaps three hours at the most. His contacts had led him to believe that the Earl of Manchester would be quartered in Horncastle that same night and so he had been quite unprepared to find the enemy occupying the town. It had taken him the whole evening to evade numerous troops coming and going from villages around Horncastle, unsure of the safety of his mission in these conditions, he had laid low until the activities quietened.

The messenger, one of Lord Fairfax's trusted officers, explained why his Lordship's expected attack on the enemy siegeworks near Hull had not taken place. At daybreak on Monday, some of the Earl of Newcastle's forces had attacked Ragged Jetty, one of Hull's own defence outworks, and a place of great importance for Parliamentarian ships needing to ride safely in the Humber, close to Hull. The defenders of Ragged Jetty, expecting Lord Fairfax's soldiers to join them that morning, supposed these forces to be friendly and allowed them to get too near before realising that they were Royalists. Luckily there was another of Hull's defence works close by which the guards managed to alert and the enemy were beaten out of Ragged Jetty, leaving behind them many of their soldiers and officers dead or injured as they retreated.

The officer ended his confidential report with an important

communication. Lord Fairfax had called a Council of War where it had been resolved that the defenders of Hull would fall out of the city, in two separate bodies, and attack the enemy at nine o'clock on Wednesday morning, the 11th October.

Well pleased with his news, the Earl gave orders for the messenger to be cared for and then retired to his bed, hoping for sleep to overtake him before the daylight came. It was close to morning before the very last of his outlying troops managed to assemble at the alarm place, wounded, hungry and in an exhausted condition they collapsed into the camp where they found food and care awaiting them and their tired horses.

Wednesday morning dawned bright and cold, bringing with it a new optimism clearly felt by all those who had been lucky enough to sleep during the restless night. Preparations were quickly under way for moving out of Bolingbroke while the Royalists in the castle watched and pondered over the reasons for this move. Why were the Parliamentarians leaving? Was Henderson on his way to the castle, and if so, were they running from him?

It took most of the morning to pack up, load the carts and assemble all regiments so that it was almost mid-day before the cavalry began to move away from Horncastle Hill, leaving the infantry to follow on as soon as they could. All regiments and companies had received the day's new password of 'Truth and Peace' before the Earl set out with his cavalry intending to supervise the new quarters himself and seek out the best possible site for his men to face the Royalists when they arrived.

Yesterday's journey back from Horncastle had enabled him to take a good look around the hills at suitable ground and he was anxious to move up there, nearer to Horncastle if there was sufficient time. It was a better day, a fresh wind had blown all the mist away and the sun was bright overhead as they rode towards Winceby. In advance of the cavalry and on each flank of them rode the look-outs, primed to bring early warning of the enemy's movements.

Manchester and his officers were now quite certain that the Royalists were more than eager to catch up with the Association army and destroy them. Recent encounters must have exacerbated their contempt, re-assuring them of an easy victory once a stand was made.

The cavalry had passed by the village area of Winceby, and were just about to begin the final ascent on to the Wolds when the scouts came racing back with urgent news for the Earl. The Royalists had been sighted on the hilltop. At first it was assumed that they too were a scouting party, but on drawing nearer, the Earl's scouts realised that Henderson was advancing towards Bolingbroke castle with all his forces.

Once again the Earl found himself in a difficult situation, for the second time in two days the enemy had inconveniently arrived before he was prepared for them! A halt was called while the senior officers joined with the Earl to discuss the possibilities of their situation. It was not a good place to fight, and yet Bolingbroke was even worse, too far away now for the cavalry to risk being routed should they attempt to return.

21. *Although the surface terrain has altered in the past three hundred and fifty years the under-lying contours have not. This photograph, taken with a telephoto-lens lens from a similar position to that used for 4a, shows the probable position of the first sighting of the Royalists on the skyline. The open area shown (and continuing to both left and right) is the only area which could have accommodated the numbers of troops known to have been drawn-up and involved.*

Manchester's infantry were too far behind to be of any immediate assistance so the cavalry would have to bear the full weight of attack. Because his own troops, and many of the others, were still not fully recovered from the previous day's travelling, Colonel Cromwell dismissed any thoughts of making an uphill charge upon the enemy. The long, steep incline was indented with craggs and littered with sandstone boulders large enough to provide the Royalist dragoons with positions for defensive fire-cover. Rough ground and stone fragments would create stumbling-blocks for any tired, unwary horse attempting this climb. Athough the situation looked desperate Fairfax declared that his troops would manage the charge, 'They always manage to fight harder and longer when the odds are against them.' Other officers agreed that the time had now come to make a stand, even if the ground was not good.

Reluctant to commit himself, the Earl looked around in search of a better plan. Amongst the trees to the right of them was a deep valley, or ravine, while the ground to their left was saturated by overflowing becks, behind them and nearer to the village, the road had passed over a small, open plain situated in the middle of two slopes. This seemed to be the only reasonable ground to fight on, although the enemy would have to be coaxed into leaving their lofty hilltop. The Royalists occupied a strong, defensive position on top of the hill, but they were also poised ready and quivering to attack the minute the Association cavalry retreated. Manchester knew that as soon as they turned back to reach the plain, his men would inevitably become disorganised and an easy prey to rout.

Cromwell's own troops were already practised in the art of carrying out an organised retreat. They had suddenly come face to face with the Earl of Newcastle, General Goring, Lord Eythin and the bulk of the Royalists' Northern Army on the outskirts of Gainsborough the previous July. Cromwell had soon realised that a retreat was inevitable and so detailed his cousin, Major Whalley, and Captain Ayscoughe to hold their troops and detain the enemy while the rest of the cavalry got away. A successful retreat had been made possible by the two officers taking it in turns to stand and hold the enemy, repeating this disciplined manoevre for eight or nine removes

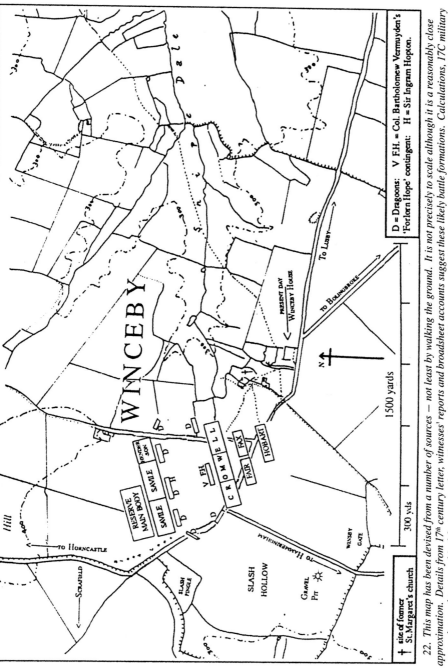

22. This map has been devised from a number of sources — not least by walking the ground. It is not precisely to scale although it is a reasonably close approximation. Details from 17th century letter; witnesses' reports and broadsheet accounts suggest these likely battle formations. Calculations, 17C military procedure and topographical features need consideration when placing the tableau on a map. Although, over the past 350 years, drainage and agriculture have altered the superficial features of the terrain the basic contours are unchanged.

D = Dragoons: V F.H. = Col. Bartholomew Vermuyden's
'Forlorn Hope' contingent: H = Sir Ingram Hopton.

1500 yards

300 yds

✝ = site of former
St.Margaret's church

77.

until the retreat was complete.

It was well worth another try. To the watching Royalists, the anticipated enemy retreat looked set to take place below them as Cromwell's men, seeming tired and reluctant to fight, slowly edged backwards. Behind these, the rest of the Association cavalry were falling back, as if preparing for a dash back to Boston.

The temptation proved irresistible: Manchester's Foot regiments were still nowhere in sight and his cavalry seemed unwilling to fight without their support. With shouts of 'Cavendish' the leading Royalist dragoons started down the hill in triumph, closely followed by more troops equally keen to exact vengeance on a cowardly enemy. Suddenly, the Association horse halted and wheeled about to face them, standing resolute and menacing with their pistols and swords at the ready, they held their ground as the leading Royalists reined in their horses and came to a stop – on equal ground, but very, very close.

Provoked into leaving their hilltop position and with the Parliamentary cavalry watching their every movement, the Royalists were now committed to fighting on lower ground. Far from their recent apparent reluctance, Cromwell's troops were cheering and keen to get started.

After a brief discussion with his senior cavalry officers the Earl of Manchester returned to fetch his infantry, intending to quicken their pace and bring them into the battle. Colonel Cromwell was entrusted with the command of Manchester's cavalry in addition to his own, and was therefore in a position to lead the first charge upon the enemy should the Earl be delayed.

The Association cavalry were divided up into six divisions, or squadrons. Because there was only sufficient ground for three of them to charge simultaneously, Fairfax's two divisions stood ready, behind Cromwell's, to make the second charge, while Sir Miles Hobart held a firm rearguard with the sixth division.

Five troops of dragoons under Vermuyden's command, were placed in front of the cavalry, one central troop to act as the Forlorn Hope and commence hostilities, a role normally undertaken by infantrymen. The other four troops were to carry out their normal dragoon activities i.e. each troop of 110 musketeers mounted on inferior, expendable horses would ride into position, dismount and throw their reins over the next horse's neck, leaving a string of ten horses to be held by the eleventh man, the horseholder. Each troop thus consisted of one hundred men standing ready to fire and ten men holding all the horses ready for further action.

On the other side of the plain, the Royalists divided up into only four divisions, three of them faced Cromwell's front ranks and the fourth squadron secured the rear. Their dragoons, placed opposite to Vermuyden's, consisted of twenty-one troops but only numbered between 700 to 800 men. Even so, they still outnumbered Vermuyden's five full troops of 550 men. Cavalry numbers appeared to work out in a similar manner with seventy-four Royalist troops facing the forty-odd Association troops of fuller ranks. When Manchester arrived with close on 1,500 foot the sides would be more even.

10.

AMES BERRY, Captain-Lieutenant of Cromwell's own troop, was well aware that his chances of coming through this battle unscathed were practically nil. The Royalists, most of all those from Gainsborough, hated him and were after his blood for slaying their Colonel, Sir Charles Cavendish. Berry knew full well their sporadic calls of 'Cavendish' were personal threats of vengeance to be exacted upon him when the fighting started. Smiling grimly, he urged his horse into position at the head of his troop, now the Colonel was in command of the cavalry and about to lead the first charge it was Berry's place to take over as captain.

When he recruited his men, Cromwell was very choosey. He picked yeomen's sons and freemen who knew what they fought for, and many who were not God-fearing and honest were rejected as unsuitable, leaving those who did qualify to feel very special indeed. As respect for these well-trained and disciplined men grew so did the honour of serving with them. For each of his troops Cromwell tried to find at least eighty good men and four commissioned officers, namely a captain, lieutenant, cornet and a quartermaster. For his own personal troop he needed a deputy to take over occasionally, and it was James Berry who became his captain-lieutenant.

Colonel Cromwell leaned forward to stroke the graceful arch of his horse's neck, it was a tall, strong animal with probably a measure of Arab blood in its veins. Height could be an advantage in battle, it enabled the rider to view the field around him and check how a battle was progressing. Turning in his saddle, Cromwell surveyed the regiments drawn up behind him. Unlike the armies of a year ago, these troops were an impressive sight and reflected money well-spent on supplies of buff coats, back and breast armour, steel hats, a pair of pistols each and good swords. Even the enemy would soon have cause to agree that these troops were a fine body of fighting men, and extraordinarily well-armed.

Regimental colours breathed identity into the assembled ranks. Recognisable were those of Manchester, Willoughby of Parham, Colonel Fleetwood, Majors Harrison, Whalley, and Rich as well as others less familiar to the assembled regiments. Tawny reds were popular and Cromwell's own distinctive colours were known to most, as were the blue of the Fairfaxes, like the deep blue field of Thomas Fairfax's own colours which were embossed with a dark blue acanthus pattern and edged by a blue and white fringe.

Normally a quiet and agreeable man, Sir Thomas Fairfax seemed to have undergone a sudden change of character while waiting for the battle to commence. Animated and restless, his dark eyes gleaming with excitement, 'Black Tom' was impatient to launch his troops into the second cavalry charge. Sir William Fairfax was by his cousin's side with their second division and both the Fairfax cousins were deeply missing the company of their loyal fighting compatriot, Sir Henry Foulis, whose funeral was being held in Boston that very day.

Sir Miles Hobart, Colonel of the Norfolk and Suffolk Horse, was with the sixth division and ready to command the third cavalry charge. He and Cromwell had met many times this summer, Hobart had been at Wisbech, Crowland, Kings Lynn and with Cromwell at Stamford and the siege of Burghley House.

Colonel Hobart had just realised that his cousin, Sir Ingram Hopton, was present amongst the Royalists on the field and also noticed that the Portington colours were amongst those displayed there. Roger, the elder of the Portington brothers was married to Sir Ingram's sister, Joanna Hopton. Sir Ralph Hopton of Armley, father of Ingram and Joanna, was the brother of Sir Miles Hobart's mother, Willoughby.

Like very many other families throughout the country, the cousins stood and faced each other across a battlefield.

*   *   *   *   *   *

On the other side of the battlefield and in the forefront of the Royalist ranks (whose password today was 'Newcastle'), three of Newcastle's commanders were waiting for the moment to attack. The tallest of these men was Sir William Widdrington, knight, colonel of dragoons and trusted friend of the Earl of Newcastle. A large proportion of the Royalist dragoons were Widdrington's own men.

The professional Scottish soldier, Sir John Henderson, knight, was busy watching the enemy ranks and colours lining up against them, Henderson's division was drawn up on the left wing and had a total of eight troops which included those of James King (now Lord Eythin and Lieutenant-General of Newcastle's army), when Eythin returned north with the Earl to begin the siege of Hull, he left his own Horse with Henderson in Newark to assist in the fight for Lincolnshire.

Sir William Savile of Thornhill, near Dewsbury, and an adversary of the Fairfaxes during the Yorkshire fighting, commanded two of the four Royalist divisions. Unfortunately, Sir William was known to have a bad temper, was fault-finding and often showed a lack of respect for his superiors' orders. Savile's second division was placed on the right, front wing, leaving his main body to hold the central position next to Henderson. Behind these, a fourth division containing Lincolnshire troops completed the Royalist battle formation.

Amongst the dragoon leaders standing by for Widdrington's command signal, was Sir Ingram Hopton, knight, of Leathley in Yorkshire. He had served with Savile's trained bands before the war and was not only his colonel of dragoons, but also a friend, having supported Savile in his (unsuccessful) 1640 election bid as M.P. for the county. Recently, on his march south, Sir Ingram had visited Savile at Sheffield Castle, where he'd promised to spend a day 'celebrating with his friends before continuing his journey into Lincolnshire'.

There was still no sight of Manchester's Infantry and so the Royalists were anxious to begin the hostilities before the Earl could arrive on the field. Further delay was unreasonable, for both sides had completed their troop arrangements and the enemy's leisurely preparation for combat had only served to whip the Royalist troops into a frenzy of impatience. Cromwell knew that no further advantage could be gained by delay, it was time now for him to take up his position to lead the first cavalry charge into action.

In the final moments before battle, the troopers on each side passed the time with their usual scrutiny of each other's colours, a 'who's who' and 'where are they' identification parade. Taunts echoed back and forth across the field, cries of 'traitors', 'rebels', 'cowards' and 'papists' were some of the lesser offensive names although the venom that accompanied these calls left no doubt about their scorn. Across the field, the Lincolnshire Royalists of Sir William Pelham and Sir Robert Dallison's cavalry carried on a bitter exchange with the Lincolnshire Parliamentarians of Sir Anthony Irby and Lord Willoughby of Parham's dragoons. Troopers of Savile and Fairfax's cavalry, old enemies from Yorkshire, glared at each other while waiting for the chance to resume their interrupted combat in a different county.

Suddenly the noise subsided, leaving a few desultory shouts to trail away as a hush descended over the assembled armies. Someone, somewhere at the front, had spotted the first intimation that the battle was about to begin and tension flashed like wildfire through all the ranks. It seemed as though thousands of men held their breath while they watched and waited, only the crows, who no longer bothered about the activities below them, carried on with their compulsive chattering.

A mighty roar drowned the sound of trumpets. Colonel Bartholemew Vermuyden led the first attack with his Forlorn Hope against Sir William Widdrington and so the dragoons began their race to find the protection of some cover where they could dismount and be ready to fire at the enemy cavalry. The unexpected bursts of musket fire from the Forlorn Hope sent the crows flapping out of the trees in a panic, screaming as they circled high in the air above their territory.

When the dragoons of both sides had completed their

opening volley, it was time for the leading cavalry divisions to charge across the field and begin close combat with their opposite numbers. Cromwell had the troopers drawn up in close order ranks, which meant that there were no gaps left between the horses for the enemy to slip through; when each cavalryman kept his right knee locked against the left thigh of his neighbour, it presented the enemy with an impenetrable wall bearing down upon him. Timing the charge was of the utmost importance for the cavalry who had to ride past, or through the dragoons between each fusillade, hoping to be out of range before they loaded and fired again. Cromwell waited until the first dragoon volley had finished and then, with trumpets blaring and his troopers chanting their favourite battle hymn, he spurred his horse into action and led his three divisions into the assault.

It was a near fatal disaster for he miss-timed the charge. Savile's dragoons led by Colonel Ingram Hopton, acted so rapidly that they fired their second shot in half the normal time and met Cromwell head on. Seeing a dragoon raise his musket towards him and take aim, Cromwell urged his horse forward and struck at the man with his sword, but it was too late for the musket fired and his horse took the full blast of the shot under its jaw, the musket ball lodged in the horse's brain and killed it instantly.

As soon as he heard the shot and felt his horse stumble, Cromwell knew that he must throw himself clear prior to its dead body ploughing on into a group of enemy dragoons. He hit the ground seconds before the horse fell but just as he staggered to his feet ready to defend himself, Hopton's mount charged at him and sent him sprawling again. Shaken and dazed, Cromwell looked up from the ground into the nozzle of a pistol and heard Sir Ingram call on him to surrender, then saw him topple from his horse as the cavalry fell in and combat began. Looking around him for a horse, Cromwell hurriedly seized one of the dragooners' mounts and plunged back into the fighting.

With Henderson in command, the Royalist left wing charged into the field and proceeded to take full advantage of the mêlée created by Colonel Hopton's dragoons. The initial charge, although disordered by Cromwell's fall, was soon corrected and both sides fought well, each firmly holding their own ground and resisting the other's attempts to break through. Dragoons on foot raced for whatever cover was available on the flanks and then concentrated their musket-fire at the enemy cavalry as they fought.

Because of Colonel Hopton's timely intervention, Sir William Savile's main division was spared the full brunt of Cromwell's first attack and so managed to hold their ground. As soon as Cromwell became mobile again they were vulnerable for he had already interpreted his recent deliverance as a sign of the Almighty's approval, and nothing would stop him now. At first there was an initial resistance to the onslaught, but before long Cromwell detected early signs of the enemy's instability and encouraged his men to redouble their efforts. Taking stock of the situation he assessed the weakness of Savile's flank and organised a decisive thrust against that area. Now it was time for the second cavalry charge to come in.

Fairfax and his two restless divisions had been smouldering with pent-up energy while they waited for the signal to charge. Inspite of the dramatic start, when it seemed that Cromwell had been killed and the Royalists of the left wing had stalled their attackers, fighting during the last fifteen minutes appeared to have become more stabilised with neither side giving much ground.

A cheer had gone up from the Parliamentary ranks when Cromwell, apparently uninjured, was seen to mount a horse and take his revenge on the enemy. Henderson was also exposed to danger when his own horse was killed beneath him and the Royalist had to fight on foot until re-mounted. When Fairfax's trumpeters responded to a signal for the second charge, his cavalry immediately shot forward in a frenzied onslaught upon Savile's two divisions.

The sight of Fairfax's aggressive cavalry racing towards them was enough to dishearten all but the most seasoned of fighters. But Savile's own officers were late in giving their call to stand and fight. After enduring seconds of indecision many of the the troops took a distant call of 'Faces about' as an order to be obeyed with alacrity – and turned to run! Fairfax's troops hit the disordered flanks of the Royalists with such force that the remains of Savile's main body reeled backwards into the ranks of their own fourth division, causing such chaos that the whole army began to retreat in panic. They were instantly put to rout.

The Royalists retreated back up the very same hill that they had descended in such triumph a little earlier. A bottleneck was soon caused by the great numbers of fleeing troops converging on the hill and trying to outrun the cavalry of Fairfax and Hobart. Keeping to the lane meant certain death for the Royalists, there were bodies of the dead and wounded lying all along the length of the blood-soaked highway. Pockets of resistance were soon overcome, once their pistols were fired there was no time to prime them, the weapon was then used as a club or hurled in the adversary's face before resorting to the sword. Fairfax's men closed in on their prey, daring to 'touch' with their pistols in order to make each shot count, a necessity learnt in their Yorkshire campaigns.

The hillsides around Winceby reverberated with the terrible clamour of battle. As the sound of musket fire cleared, sudden, piercing screams of the wounded and dying took over, with the full-throated roars and shouts of the fighting men as they gave vent to their triumph and anger, or occasional dismay. Shrill cries from the wounded horses infected many of the younger, nervous mounts with a frenzied terror that set them to rearing and neighing in the very midst of the action. Those troopers who became unhorsed ran down towards the swollen rivers, hoping to hide amongst the reeds, many were drowned when the weight of their armour pushed them down into the mud. Some tried to slash their way through the boundary hedges, while others spurred panic-stricken horses into jumping the obstacles only to become firmly stuck in a quagmire on the other side. Several tried to cut across Scrafield, but the water rushing down from the hills swept the fugitives off their feet as they hurriedly tried to release the leather fasteners of their heavy back and breast plates.

When the Royalist retreat was under way and the fighting gradually moved further afield it seemed, in the now uncontested areas of the battlefield, that the very earth itself

23. A view from the south with (the present-day) Winceby House in the distance. Slash Hollow is out of the picture to the left on the other side of the Hammeringham road. This field was 'below' the battle at the outset but, being downhill, would be a likely direction for attempting to escape the battle when once fleeing. The 'Winsby gate' seems likely to have been at the foot of this field close to the position from which this photograph was taken. Slash Lane runs approximately on the skyline.

was writhing and moaning in agony. In contrast to the dead, who laid quiet and very, very still, the wounded felt their bodies contort with pain, bringing involuntary screams to their lips as they moved or tried to sit up. There were so many of them. Some held out their arms and cried for help, imploring God for mercy, some cursed him violently as they coughed up blood or mourned over their mutilated limbs. A few of the wounded managed to stagger a short distance before they fell again, dazed and weak from loss of blood.

Here and there amongst the dying horses, one of the animals would make a last desperate but futile effort to stand and join a group nearby that was grazing quietly, seemingly oblivious to the carnage all around.

Seconds later the destruction began again – the infantry had arrived at last.

11.

AFTER THE BATTLE

'. . . making good the field . . .'

L EAVING THE FAIRFAXES and Sir Miles Hobart's divisions to chase and deal with the retreating Royalists, Colonel Cromwell remained behind at Winceby with his troops in order to capture the few remaining enemy units who were still skirmishing on the higher ground. Several of these units, like two troops belonging to Sir William Pelham of Brocklesby, had found their retreat blocked by the accumulation of Savile's cavalry withdrawing from Winceby. Captain William Westlyd, of Grimsby, and Captain Husthwaite Wright from Stalling-borough, found themselves trapped on the hill and so both troops were forced to accept quarter and reluctantly surrendered their colours to the Association cavalry. Both troop's cornets, Thomas Westlyd and Thomas Waters, attempted to break the staves of their colours before releasing them.

The Earl of Manchester arrived on the battlefield with his infantry to find that, although the battle seemed to be over, there were many prisoners to be taken. Surging onto the field, the infantry proceeded to wreak havoc and in their fury they killed 'more than they should have done' for the enemy were ready to surrender. On some occasions they even killed each other when the 'word' was either forgotten or not believed, and most of them were in a mind to pillage the bodies. There was plenty for the soldiers to do in the time left before darkness fell. As well as taking prisoners, there were hundreds of loose horses to be rounded up while a huge amount of arms and armour had been dumped and lay scattered for miles around.

Most of the Royalist dragoons had been left behind, marooned on foot when their horses dispersed leaving them to escape as best they could. Some had tried to take shelter in the village as the sounds of shots and screams were presently proving. The thatched roof of the little church was on fire, smothering the village with clouds of thick, black smoke. Some of the cottage roofs also were burning while the soldiers searched in the devastated village for escaping Royalists.

In order to avoid contact with either the cavalry or the infantry, or drown in the rivers and marshy land, there was really only one direction left for the Royalist dragoons to take and that was southwards. It meant running across the open ground near a hollow to reach the boundary gate into Hammeringham village. The woodland of the pringles and holts was useless anyway, already full of fugitives who were certain to be discovered very soon by Manchester's soldiers.

Chased by the avenging Parliamentarians, large numbers of Royalist dragoons made a headlong dash for the boundary gate and the inevitable happened, scores of them reached the gateway at the same moment and effectively managed to block the exit. Tragically, the boundary gate did not open into Hammeringham. Known as the 'WINSBY gate', it opened into Winceby *from* the village of Hammeringham and it was therefore impossible for the dragoons to pull the gate towards them because of the numbers pushing against it. With dozens of their men still arriving, the pressure increased on those at the front who were suffocated and trampled over, then, while frantically attempting to claw their way over the gate, the Royalist dragoons were attacked from behind and massacred.

Some of the wounded Royalists managed to crawl away and hide in the rivers, only to drown there; one hundred injured men were able to find a gravel pit close-by where they hid, some breathing their last as they lay inside the pit.

When the Earl inspected the field he was deeply shocked by the carnage and destruction. Calling for the killing to cease and prisoners to be taken care of, he was especially mindful of the appeals made to him by some of the mortally wounded adversaries. It had affected him deeply, for he saw the truth of their words when they protested about the massacres and said to him:

'The Commission of Array brought us here full sore against our wills, we were as true servants to the Parliament, to our Religion and Liberties as any in England, and woe to those that were the cause that Lincolne and Yorkshire became a prey to the enemy, and that the friends of the Parliament have been neglected, we die, we die as true friends to the Parliament as any.'

Suddenly it became too dark to continue searching the hedges and woods, the Earl and his senior officers retired to Horncastle for the night followed by the exhausted cavalry who returned to their quarters in the villages. Miles Hobart and the Fairfaxes also returned to Horncastle after their pursuit of the enemy having scattered the countryside for miles around with dead and dying Royalists. The Infantry were quartered in and around Horncastle where the wounded were cared for and the prisoners held. Winceby was left under guard that night, until the officers could return at daybreak to assess the victory.

Although wounded, James Berry had somehow managed to survive the battle, Cromwell's regimental surgeon attended to the wound and declared that his patient would not be out of action for long. It seemed incredible that the Parliamentarians had suffered so few casualties, there was talk of ten men killed and fifty wounded but no officers other than Berry. A miracle indeed.

*   *   *   *   *   *

In the cold light of early morning, Winceby field brought a shudder of horror to even the most experienced witness. The living needed to survive and so nothing was wasted, shirts, boots, buffcoats, even jewellery and money were skillfully found and removed. All the dead had been stripped naked leaving their pathetic, white bodies sprawled awkwardly on the ground, seeming unreal and out of place in the open air. Horse carcasses lay stiff-legged and lifeless, looking like wooden models waiting to be placed upright again on their outstretched legs. Walking amongst the piles of bodies, searching for relatives and old friends was a gory business for already the carrion crows had arrived to scavenge amongst the dead, becoming gorged and reluctant to fly away as the living approached them.

Sir Miles Hobart had come to look for his cousin. Accompanied by Cromwell and a small party of soldiers, they all picked their way carefully over the field towards the place where Cromwell's horse had fallen, then Colonel Hobart dismounted and called for the soldiers to come and search amongst a heap of corpses lying nearby. Thankfully, it was not long before they found Sir Ingram Hopton, the gentry seemed to be quickly identified by their fair skins contrasting oddly with the more tanned and rugged bodies of the other ranks.

Sir Ingram had died where he'd fallen, almost at the exact spot where Cromwell had looked up into his pistol barrel and it was difficult to connect this bloody corpse with the dashing, brave Colonel Hopton of yesterday's battle. Cromwell turned quickly, disgusted by the results of pillaging, and ordered the soldiers to wrap the body in a blanket before conveying it to St. Mary's Church, in Horncastle, for an honourable burial.

The infantry continued with the grisly work of collecting corpses and transporting them on wagons to the burial pits, the already established gravel pit proving to be a natural asset and large enough to acommodate a great number. The number of dead was at first judged to be around 300, but it soon became clear that there were many more to be found on the highways and in the rivers, bringing the total nearer to 500. One fatally wounded soldier, Miles Hope, managed to escape and crawl as far as Hagworthingham before he died and was buried in the churchyard there.

Arms and armour numbering in the region of 1500 pieces had been collected and piled onto carts: these, and almost 2,000 horses rounded up, became the bonus of the day. Colonel Hobart stayed for a while seeking news of his cousin Joanna's husband, Roger, and his brother Robert Portington. Although there was news that Robert had been wounded in the arm, he was not amongst the 800 prisoners despatched to Boston that day for transport to London by sea. Not finding the Portingtons amongst the dead or the prisoners, Hobart went on to join the Earl of Manchester who had just arrived.

Manchester had news for them.

A messenger had just arrived from Hull with news of yet another great victory. Yesterday, Wednesday, the 11th October, Lord Fairfax and Sir John Meldrum had sallied out from the west gates of Hull with 1500 men in order to attack the Royalists, having first tricked the enemy into believing the attack would be from the north side. The assault had gone well for them until reinforcements arrived for the Royalists who then pushed their attackers back to the gates of the city. Hull's governor rallied his men, making them renew their efforts to beat the enemy out of the western siege-works, with such success that many guns were captured and dragged into the city that night, including one of the 'great' guns.

The burst of cheering was stopped by Manchester who held up his his hand and declared that there was yet more good news.

A Royalist messenger carrying a letter from Widdrington to the Earl of Newcastle had been taken prisoner near Hull, the captured letter told of the disaster that had over-taken the Royalist forces at Winceby. News later reached the Earl of Newcastle of his army's defeat at Winceby and the serious blow that it dealt their plans to capture Lincolnshire. During the night, he abandoned his siege of Hull and retired north again.

Hull was saved.

Such a roar of cheering and shouting went up that people came running to them from all directions to see what the good news was about, the soldiers slapped each other on the back, trumpeters dashed away to take the news to other units in the area and drummers began excited drumrolls. The horrors of the recent battle faded rapidly, talk of death and war was ousted by the exciting turn of events and promises of future victories.

The Eastern Association had established itself as a force to be reckoned with. From Winceby they could move on to clear the Royalists from all Lincolnshire, there was Lincoln to re-capture as well as the towns of Newark and Gainsborough, and who knows, even help to regain Yorkshire.

Wandering amongst the ruins of their village, the families of Winceby saw how much work they had to do before the winter arrived. New roofs were needed for the church, the parsonage, and for several homes that were still smouldering; some of the barns would need rebuilding while others had escaped with minor damage.

Thomas Page was relieved to see that both the haywain and the plough he had inherited from his father remained intact. The village might suffer changes but the land was still here. It would support them again next year, the year after that and in all of the years to come.

There was no time just now to stop and think about politics, battles and death. The living had to be fed, housed, and taken care of, there were plans to be made and too much work to do.

*　　*　　*　　*　　*　　*

Perhaps one day, someone would find the time
to remember the dead.

24. There is now no church in Winceby — these few graves mark the 19th century churchyard where St. Margaret's church once stood.

UP TO NASEBY BATTLE (1645)

1599 ... Apr 25	Born at Huntingdon. .... (d. Sept 3 1658)	
1603 ...	Death of Q. Elizabeth 1 = Acc. of James 1.	
1616 ... Apr 23	Cromwell goes to Sidney Sussex College, Cambridge.	
...	Death of Shakespeare.	
1617 ... Jun	Death of father; Cromwell leaves college.	
1620 ... Aug 22	Marries Elizabeth Bourchier at St Giles, London.	
1621 ...	Robert is born .... (d. 1637 aged 16)	
1623 ...	Oliver Jnr is born .... (d. 1644 aged 21)	
1624 ...	Bridget is born .... (d. 1662)	
1625 ...	Death of James 1. Acc. of Charles 1.	
1626 ...	Richard is born .... (d. 1671)	
1628 ...	Henry is born .... (d. 1674)	
... Mar	Enters House of Commons as as M.P.	
... May	Petition of Rights.	
1629 ...	Elizabeth (Bettie) is born .. (d. 6 Aug 1958)	
... Mar	Dissolution of Parliament by Charles 1.	
1631 ...	Cromwell family move to St. Ives.	
1632 ...	James born .... and .... dies .... (d. 1632)	
1636 ...	Cromwell family move to Ely.	
1637 ...	Mary is born .... (d. 1713)	
... Nov	Ship-money case against John Hampden.	
...	Death of Robert aged 16 yrs.	
1638 ...	Frances is born .... (d. 1721)	
1639 ... Apr	Short Parliament. M.P. for Cambs.	
... Nov	Long Parliament. M.P. for Cambs again.	
1641 ... Oct	Irish Massacres.	
... Nov 27	Grand Remonstrance.	
1642 ... Jan	Five Members escape arrest by the King, who leaves London.	
...	Cromwell a Capt. of Troop No 67 under Essex.	
...	Son Oliver a Cornet under Capt St John - No 8 Troop.	
...	Cromwell saves Cambridge Plate for .... Parliament.	
... Aug 22	King raises Standard at Nottingham.	
... Oct 23	Battle of Edgehill.	
1643 ... Mar	Cromwell has five troops.	
... Jul 28	Battle of Gainsboro. Cromwell Governor of Ely.	
... Aug	Manchester commands Eastern Association.	
... Sep	Siege of Hull. Cromwell has ten troops.	
...	Lincolnshire joins the Eastern Association.	
...	Parliament accepts Scottish Solemn League & Covenant.	
... Oct 11 BATTLE OF WINCEBY		
... Oct 27	Newcastle becomes a Marquis.	
1644 ... Jan 23	Cromwell made Lt.-General.	
... Apr	Cromwell has a full Regiment of 14 troops.	
...	Death of son Oliver aged 21.	
... Jul 2	Battle of Marston Moor.	
... Oct 27	2nd Battle of Newbury.	
... Dec 9	Self-denying Order proposed.	
1645 ... Jun 14	Battle of Naseby.	

SEPT./OCTOBER, 1643

Sat	Sept 2	Siege of Hull begins.
Mon	Sept 4	William Harlakenden has dinner with Cromwell at Ely.
Tue	Sept 5	Cromwell leaves Ely for Boston.
Sat	Sept 9	Letter from Manchester says 'most of his horse & dragoons sent to Cromwell'.
Mon	Sept 11	Cromwell at Boston – with Willoughby of Parham.
Thu	Sept 14	Fairfax floods areas around Hull.
Sat	Sept 16	Kings Lynn capitulates to Manchester.
Mon	Sept 18	Troops at Boston leave for Barton on Humb
Wed	Sept 20	Lincolnshire added to Eastern Association.
Fri	Sept 22	A 'fast' day at Hull, Cromwell there.
Sat	Sept 23	Willoughby in Hull.
Sun	Sept 24	Yorkshire cavalry crossing the Humber.
Mon	Sept 25	Cromwell and Fairfax's cavalry begin journey to Boston.
Tue	Sept 26	Royalists attempt to get between their prey and Boston.
Wed	Sept 27	Cromwell and Fairfax attacked near edge of Holland. Near Horncastle?
Thu	Sept 28	All at Boston – Cromwell writes letters.
Fri	Sept 29	Royalist Magazine at Cottingham, near Hull, blown up.
Sat	Sept 30	Letter says 'Capt from Cromwell stayed lately 3 days in Hull'.
Mon	Oct 2	Cromwell in Kings Lynn and later at Ely.
Tue	Oct 3	At Ely, visits the garrison and signs letter for Ireton who is Cromwell's deputy commander there. Leaves for King's Lyn
Wed	Oct 4	Manchester moves the army to Boston.
Thu	Oct 5	Meldrum and 750 men arrive in Hull.
Fri	Oct 6	Cromwell at Boston. News leaked to enemy of impending attack on Bolingbroke Castl
Sat	Oct 7	Fairfax at Horncastle: his troops quartered i the surrounding villages.
Mon	Oct 9	Eastern Association Army move from Bosto to Stickney. Major Knight summoned the Royalists in Bolingbroke castle to surrend Attack on Hull by Newcastle.
Tue	Oct 10	Cromwell and Manchester arrive at Kirkby. Fairfax has trouble near Horncastle.
Wed	Oct 11	Manchester moves the army away from Bolingbroke. Meets Royalists at Winceby and battle ensues. Hull fights to end siege and captures the 'big' guns. Newcastle raises siege and leaves Hull during the nig
Thu	Oct 12	Association army at Horncastle. 800 prison sent to Boston. Manchester writes to the House of Lords.

At the time of WINCEBY battle: (11.10.1643)
CROMWELL was 44 years old and his home was
Ely. Married to Elizabeth for 23 yrs . . . three so
alive (had had five); Oliver 20 yrs; Richard 17 y
Henry 15 yrs. Had four daughters alive; Bridg
19 yrs; Elizabeth 14 yrs; Mary 6 yrs; Frances 5 yrs

INVENTORY OF JOHN PAGE

June, 1628

****

****

A true and perfect Inventory of the goodes & chattels of John Page layt of Winceby in the Countie of Lincoln deceased, priced the second day of June in the yeare of our Lord, 1628, by them whose names are underwritten

Imprimis his purse and apparell	£10		
Item a silver tunn, a silver salt, & a dozen of spoones	£6		
Item certaine bokes		13s	4d
Item forme in the chamber and burnt	£7		
Item four beds, with the furniture	£12		
Item two beds for servants, with their furniture		20s	
Item one trunke of linnen	£4		
Item one livery cupboard, a chest, & two stooles		10s	
Item three chests & a warming pan		20s	
Item two tables, a forme, & four buffet stooles		34s	
Item one cupboard, three chaires		26s	8d
Item half a dozen of cushions		12s	
Item one bord, a forme, & two chaires		7s	
Item a little square table & other things in the hall		22s	
Item six barrels & other utensils belonging to the buttery		20s	
Item one lead & other vessels belonging to the back house		26s	4d
Item one chearne & other things belonging to the dairy		30s	
Item brass & pewter	£3	14s	
Item four spitts & other things belonging to the kitchen		20s	
Item painted cloths about the house		3s	4d
Item bacon		20s	
Item all the graine growing in the fields	£50		
Item the sheepe	£61		
Item the horses	£23		
Item Oxen	£24	10s	
Item young beast & calves	£22	10s	
Item eight kine	£23	10s	
Item one Bull		40s	
Item one lame Oxe	£3		
Item the swine	£3	10s	
Item the waine & waine geares, plough & plough gears & all other implements of husbandry	£6		
Item the debts owed by Bills & bonds, or otherwise	£60	7s	6d
Item the pullen in the yard, & other implements unpriced		20s	

Sum total   £337 6s 2d

Praised by William more, Robert Clarke, William Barrat and William Weston

In the name of God Amen the eighteenth day of January in this year of our Lord one thousand six hundred and sixty nine. I Thomas Page of Winsby in the County of Lincoln husbandman, weak in body but of perfect remembrance laud and praise be to Almighty God doe make this my last will and testament in manner and forme following. First I bequeath my soule to Allmighty God trusting to be saved onely by the Meritts of Jesus Christ my Redeemer and my body to the christian Buriall appointed for the dead in sure and certaine hope of Resurrection to life immortal. All my worldy goods I give and bequeath in manner following. Item. I give unto Thomas Page my sonne Thirty pounds in money or gold to be sett out at a reasonable rate by my supervisors instruction and to be payd unto him within eight months after my decease. Item. I give unto William Page my sonne twelve pence. Item. I give unto John Page my sonne Thirty pounds in money or gold to be payd unto him within eighteen months after my decease the goods to be sett out at a reasonable rate as aforesaid. Item. I give unto Nathaniel my sonne Thirty pounds in money or gold to be payd unto him within three years after my decease the goods to be sett out at a reasinable rate as aforesaid; and if it shall please God that any one of my three sonnes Thomas, John or Nathaniel shall depart this life before the tyme limmited that they are to receive their legacies that then my will is his or their legacies to be divided to him or them according to my instructions and supervisors descretion. Item. I give unto John Hasell my sonne in Law twelve pence and to his wife five shillings. Item. I give unto Catharine Pearson my grandchild one ewe and a lambe. Item. I give unto Robert Pearson my grandchild one ewe lambe. Item. I give unto Susan Page my grandchild Ten shillings. Item. I give unto the poor of Winsby five shillings. I give unto the Church of Winsby three shillings and four pence. Item. I make choice of Christopher Clarke of Mavis Enderby and Thomas Clarke of Winsby to be supervisors of this my last will and testament and I doe give unto them twelve pence apiece. All the rest of my goods and chattells moveable and immovable whatsoever except before excepted I give and bequeath unto Anne Page my wife and I doe make her my sole executrixt of this my last will and testament

Thos: Page Senior

Christopher Clarke
Thomas Clarke

In the name of God amen the Tenth of Aprill in the yeare of our Lord God One Thousand six Hundred seventy and nine I Ann Page of Winceby in the County Lincoln Widdow sick in Body but of perfect Remembrance laud and praise to All mighty God do make this my last will and Testament in manner and forme folowing. First I bequeath my soule to allmighty God trusting to be saved only by the merits of Jesus Christ my Redemer my Body to the Christain Burial apointed for the dead in sure and certain hope of Resurrection to life Immortal. All my worldly goods I give and bequeath in manner and form following

I give unto William Page my sonn Twenty shillings
* I give unto Nathaniel Page my sonn Twenty Pounds (* crossed out – deceased)
I give unto Thomas Page my Grandchild Twenty shillings
I give unto Susanna Page my Grandchild Twenty shillings
I give unto Ann Page my Grandchild Twenty shillings
I give unto Elizabeth Page my daughter in law Twenty shillings
I give unto Robert Pearson my grandchild Twenty shillings
I give unto Kathrin Pearson my grandchild Twenty shillings

I give unto the poore of Winceby Three shillings four pence
I give unto the Church of Winceby Three shillings four pence

All the rest of my worldly goods and chattells moveable and immoveable except what before excepted or what kind soever they do ( ) to get ( ) ( ) ( ) I give to my two sonns Thomas Page and John Page and I do make them my Whole executors of this my last will and Testament

and I do make choyce of Christopher Clarke of Mavis Enderby and Thomas Clarke of Winceby to be my supervisors of this my last Will and testament and I give to other of them Twelve pence

her   mark
Ann Page

Anne Page
William Clark   his mark
John Hall   William Page

APPENDIX 5.

Inventory of Thomas Page   March the iith 1672
*****************************   **********************

A true and perfect Inventorie of all the goods and chattells of Thomas Page of Winsbie (   )
lately deceased prized and vallued by us whose names are under written

	£	s	d
Imprimis his purse and apparrell	5	0	0
In the haule one long table one forme two chaires			
one liverie cubbert one square table two framed stooles }	1	13	4
In the parlor one tresl bed with alle the furniture thereto belonging	2	13	4
Three other beds in the same parlour with there furniture belonging to them	4	0	0
three chaiyrs in the same room		16	0
In the parlour chamber one bed with the furniture belonging to it	1	10	0
In the same chamber one Trunke with certain linning in it	5	0	0
In another chamber two stock beds with there furniture belonging to them	1	6	8
One silver tun & seavean silver spoons	4	0	0
In the Dayrie one chimnell one Tub with severall other nesesaries	1	5	0
Butter and cheese in the same room		10	0
Fower flickes of Bacon	1	13	4
In the kitchin one cubber one dyshbench one glascase two little tables }			
three barrells One hoghead with some other nesesaries }	1	10	0
Two peeces of puter	1	13	4
4 brass pots	2	0	0
5 brass pans	1	15	0
One warming pan one skillet two Spitts a pair of cobirons		13	4
20 quarter of Barley	12	0	0
24 quarter of Mault	16	0	0
16 quarter of Oats	5	12	0
2 quarter of Pease	1	4	0
Hay 3 loads	1	10	0
6 horses young and old	14	0	0
8 draught Oxen	30	0	0
6 Cowes	12	0	0
7 young beaste	13	6	8
6 Score Sheep young and old	20	0	0
4 Swine	2	0	0
the poultrey in yard		6	8
20 acres of tyld land	10	0	0
15 acres of hay land	5	0	0
the waine and wainegeres plow and geres with a quantie of tie	5	-	-
Sacks and Measures	00	10	0
in cloth and yarne	01	10	0
all things not prized and forgotten		5	0

       Sum total   £187 3s 8d

INVENTORY OF ANN PAGE

September 30th 1679

A true and perfect Inventory of all the goods and chattells of Ann Page of Winsby Widdow lately deceased praised and valued by us whose names are under written

		£	s	d
Impr	Her purse and aparell	1	0	0
Item	In the haule one long table one long forme two Chaires one liverie cubort one square table two framed stooles	1	13	4
Item	In the Parloure one tressle bed with all the furniture thereto belonging	2	13	4
	Three other beds in the same parlour with furniture thereto belonging	4	0	0
	Three Chaires in the same room	0	18	0
Item	In the parlour Chamber one bed with the furniture thereto belonging	1	10	0
	In the same chamber one Trunk with certaine Linen in it	4	0	0
	Another chamber two stocke beds with the furniture belonging to them	1	6	0
	One silver tun seven silver spoons	4	0	0
Item	The Dairie one Chunnell one tub with several other necessaries	1	5	0
	Butter and cheese in the same roome with one flick of bacon	0	10	0
Item	the kitching one cubort one dishbench one glasscase two little tables three barrels one hogshead with other necessaries	1	10	0
Item	eleven peeces of pewter	1	13	0
	four brasse potts	2	0	0
	five brass pans	1	15	0
	one warming pan one skillet two spitts A pair of cobirons	0	13	0
Item	fortie quarters of Barley	30	0	0
	two quarters of Pease	1	6	8
	tenn quarters of Oats	4	0	0
	twelve loads of hay	8	0	0
	thirteen horses young and oulde	20	0	0
	six oxen	22	0	0
	seven kyne	10	10	0
	eight beast coming four years ould	12	0	0
	seven beast coming two years ould	8	15	0
	two calves	1	10	0
	five shear sheep young and ould	20	0	0
	seven swine	4	0	0
	the poultry in the yard	·	15	0
	twenty acres of tilled land	6	10	0
	waine and waine gears plough and gears	4	6	8
	forks and measures	·	10	0
	all things not praised and forgotten	·	2	6
	four quarters of malt	4	0	0
	one bill	2	16	0

some tot £192. 8. 6d

[there is an error of £1.00 in this total]

Christopher Clarke
William Page
Thomas Clarke   his mark
Robert Clarke

THE HOPTON — HOBART CONNECTION

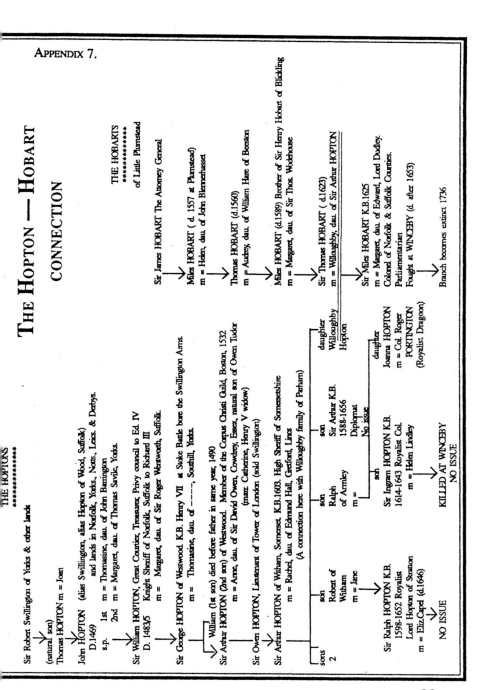

THE HOPTONS
****

Sir Robert Swillington of Yorks & other lands

(natural son)
Thomas HOPTON m = Joan

John HOPTON (alias Swillington, alias Hopton of Wood, Suffolk)
D.1469   and lands in Norfolk, Yorks, Notts, Leics. & Derbys.
s.p.   1st   m = Thomasine, dau. of John Barrington
         2nd   m = Margaret, dau. of Thomas Savile, Yorks.

Sir William HOPTON; Great Courtier, Treasurer, Privy council to Ed. IV
D. 1483/5   Knight Sheriff of Norfolk, Suffolk to Richard III
         m = Margaret, dau. of Sir Roger Wentworth, Suffolk

Sir George HOPTON of Westwood K.B. Henry VII at Stoke Battle bore the Swillington Arms.
         m = Thomasine, dau. of ------, Southill, Yorks.

William (1st son) died before father in same year, 1490
Sir Arthur HOPTON (2nd son) of Westwood. Member of the Corpus Christi Guild, Boston, 1532.
         m = Anne, dau. of Sir David Owen, Cowdrey, Essex, natural son of Owen Tudor
         (marr. Catherine, Henry V widow)

Sir Owen HOPTON, Lieutenant of Tower of London (sold Swillington)

Sir Arthur HOPTON of Witham, Somerset. K.B.1603. High Sheriff of Somersetshire
         m = Rachel, dau. of Edmund Hall, Gretford, Lincs
         (A connection here with Willoughby family of Parham)

sons
2

son
Robert of Witham
m = Jane

son
Ralph of Armley
m =

son
Sir Arthur K.B.
1588-1656
Diplomat
No issue

daughter
Willoughby Hopton

Sir Ralph HOPTON K.B.
1598-1652 Royalist
Lord Hopton of Stratton
m = Eliz Capel (d.1646)
NO ISSUE

son
Sir Ingram HOPTON K.B.
1614-1643 Royalist Col.
m = Helen Lindley
KILLED AT WINCEBY
NO ISSUE

daughter
Joanna HOPTON
m = Col Roger
PORTINGTON
(Royalist: Dragoon)

THE HOBARTS
****
of Little Plumstead

Sir James HOBART The Attorney General

Miles HOBART (d. 1557 at Plumstead)
m = Helen, dau. of John Blennerhasset

Thomas HOBART (d.1560)
m = Audrey, dau. of William Hare of Beeston

Miles HOBART (d.1589) Brother of Sir Henry Hobart of Blickling
m = Margaret, dau. of Sir Thos. Woldhouse

Sir Thomas HOBART (d.1623)
m = Willoughby, dau. of Sir Arthur HOPTON

Sir Miles HOBART K.B.1625
m = Margaret, dau. of Edward, Lord Dudley.
Colonel of Norfolk & Suffolk Counties.
Parliamentarian
Fought at WINCEBY (d. after 1653)

Branch becomes extinct 1736

SOURCES

Lincoln Archives Office
****

For Winceby

Bishops Transcripts	- MF/4/305 on microfilm
Parish Register	- 071600103A/SN070988 on microfiche
	Bapt = 1579 to 1798
	Marr = 1579 to 1798
	Bur = 1579 to 1798
Lincolnshire Wills	- George Silvester (clerk) W1631/116

John Page (yeoman)   W1628/i/167
Thomas Page (husbandman)   W1673/238
Ann Page (widow)   W1679/ii/381
Thomas Clarke (yeoman) W1683/i/78
Richard Barratt (husbn) W1667/i/123
James Burne (blacksmith)   W1687/i/83
Philip English, Snr, (husb)   W1689/i/43
Thomas Spendlaw (lab) W1687/ii/25

Inventories	- John Page	INV 133 245
	Thomas Page	INV 174 11
	Ann Page	INV 180 216

Winceby Terriers   1638 and Bundle of various dates
Faculty Papers   1865/4
Tithe Award Map
Historic Manuscript Commission Reports

         App. 7 Egerton MSS 2647 f. 229 pp 562/3/4/5/6/7
         App. 7 Egerton MSS 2647 f. 177
         App. 5 Journals of the House of Lords Vol. VI pp 255/6
         MSS of Hastings Vol II (1930)

Hill Papers 34/3	
Register of St. Mary's Church Horncastle.	1643
Register of St. Botolphs Church, Boston.	1643
Register of Hagworthingham Church	1643

Lincoln Reference Library
****

Collection of numerous Civil War Tracts and Pamphlets including
A True Relation printed Cotes, London 1643
Widdrington's letter to Newcastle, Pot Colne 12.10.1643
The Ross MSS Vol. 5

City of Hull History Library
****

Collection of numerous Civil War Tracts and Pamphlets including
Mercurius Belgicus 1646
Weekly Accompte No 7
Perfect Diurnal Sept 8th 1643
Meldrum's letter to Lenthall from Hull Oct. 1643
A True Relation by T. May
Historical Collections and private Passages of State, Vol.II
Pt. III by Rushworth (1680)
Widdrington's Letter to Newcastle, Oct. 12th. 1643
Short Memorials of Thomas Fairfax ed. by Brian Fairfax
Collection of old maps

Grimsby Reference Library
****

Microfilm Collection of 17C broadsheets including
    The Parliament Scoute
    Passages in Parliament
    The Weekly Accompte No 7
    Mercurius Aulicus
    Mercuricus Civicus
    God's Arke overtopping the waves John Vicars
    Friskney Constable's Report

Horncastle Library
****

White's Directory 1856/1882
Kelly's Directory 1930
Bishop Sutton's Register I LRS 39 (1948)
Lord Monson LRS I
Illustrated Guide to Lincolnshire Wilkinson
Bygone Lincolnshire Andrews
Horncastle or Winsby Fight Edward Lamplough
Records Historical & Antiquarian of Parishes round Horncastle by L. Conway Walter
Book of Horncastle & Woodhall Spa by David Robinson
Weir's *Horncastle*

Spilsby Library
****

'Bolingbroke Castle & the Winceby Fight' by Canon Binnall from the Old Bolingbroke Festival leaflet 1966
'A History of Bolingbroke Castle' by M.W. Thompson. Ibid.
'Old Bolingbroke' by H. Green from *Lincs Town and Village Life*
Vol. 5. and Articles in Lincoln Gazette Vol 3 1900-1909

Boston Reference Library
****

Fenland Notes and Queries
Lincolnshire Life
Victoria County History
Lincolnshire Notes & Queries
Lincolnshire Past & Present
Lincolnshire Villages by Green
Maps Collection
Directories

REFERENCE BOOKS, BIOGRAPHIES & MILITARIA
****

ABOTT W.C.	*The Writings & Speeches of Oliver Cromwell* – 4 vols.	(Cambs Mass. 1937-47)
AYLMER & MORILL	*The Civil War & Interregnum*	
BARRIFFE Col. Wm.	*Military Discipline of the Young Artillery Man*	(1661)
BELL (ed)	*Fairfax Correspondence*	(1849)
BERRY & LEE	*A Cromwellian Major General, Career of James Berry*	
BLOMEFIELD F.	*History of Norfolk* Vol.7 p.244	(1807)
BROTHERTON J	*Life of Oliver Cromwell, Lord Protector of the Commonwealth*	(1743)
BROXAP E.	*The Sieges of Hull*	
BUCHAN John.	*Oliver Cromwell*	(1934)
BURNE & YOUNG	*The Great Civil War*	(1959)
CARLYLE Thomas	*Oliver Cromwell's Letters & Speeches*, 3 vols	(1857)
CLAY J.W.	*The Gentry of Yorks at the time of the Civil War* Y.A.J .XXII	(1915)
CLIFFE J.T.	*The Yorks Gentry from the Reformation to the Civil War*	(1969)
COOKE A.M.	*St. Botolph's Town*	
CROMWELL Ass'n	*Cromwelliana*	(1976 - 1993)
CRUSO John	*Military Instructions for the Cavallrie*	(1632)
DAVIES Godfrey	*The Army of the Eastern Association*	(1931)
FIRTH C.H.	*The Raising of the Ironsides*	(1899)
FIRTH C.H.	*Cromwell's Army*	(1902)
FIRTH & DAVIES	*The Regimental History of Cromwell's Army*	(1940)
FOSTER W.E.	*The Plundered Minsters of Lincolnshire*	
FRASER Antonia	*Cromwell Our Chief of Men*	(1975)
GARDINER S.R.	*History of the Great Civil War 1642-9*	(1893)
GARNER A.A.	*Boston and the Great Civil War*	(1972)
GAUNT PETER	*The Cromwellian Gazetteer*	(1987)
GREGG Pauline	*Oliver Cromwell*	(1989)
HARDING N.S.	*Bonney's Church Notes*	(1937)
HAYTHORNTHWAITE P	*The English Civil War 1642-1651*	(1983)
HOLMES C.	*Seventeenth Century Lincolnshire*	
HOLMES C.	*The Eastern Association in the English Civil War*	(1974)
H.M.S.O.	*Newark and the Civil War*	
KINGSTON A.	*East Anglia in the Civil War*	(1897)
LAWSON Mike	*For God and the North*	(1985)
LINDLEY	*Fenland Riots and the English Revolution*	
MADDISON	*Lincolnshire Pedigrees*, p. 442, 443	
MANNING Brian	*The English People and the English Revolution*	(1991)
MARKHAM C.R.	*A Life of the Great Lord Fairfax*	(1870)
NEWMAN P.R.	*Royalist Officers in England and Wales 1642-60*	
NORTH Thomas	*The Church Bells of Lincolnshire*	
OLLARD Richard	*This War Without an Enemy*	
PARTIZAN Press	*English Civil War Notes & Queries*	(1984-93)
PEACOCK Edward	*Army Lists of the Roundheads and Cavaliers*	(1874)
PICTON	*Oliver Cromwell The Man and His Mission*	
REID Stuart	*Officers & Regiments of the Royalist Army*	
RICHARDSON John	*The Local Historian's Encyclopedia*	(1989)
RUSSELL E & R	*Old & New Landscapes in the Horncastle Area*, p. 55	(1985)
RYE Walter	*Norfolk Families*, p.350	(1913)
STEPHEN & LEE ed.	*Dictionary of National Biography*	(1921)
THOMPSON P.	*History & Antiquities of Boston*	(1856)
TOYNBEE & YOUNG	*Strangers in Oxford*	
TREASE Geoffrey	*Portrait of a Cavalier, William Cavendish, 1st Duke of Newcastle*	(1979)
VERNON John	*The Young Horseman*	(1644)
WEBSTER W. F.	*Protestation Returns 1641/Lincolnshire*	
WHITE A. J.	*Civil War Armour Find from Scrafield*	
WILSON John	*Fairfax*	(1985)